INSIDERS TALK

HOW TO GET AND KEEP YOUR FIRST LOBBYING JOB

INSIDERS TALK

HOW TO GET AND KEEP YOUR FIRST LOBBYING JOB

Preparation, Potential Employers, and First-Day Performance

ROBERT L. GUYER

LOBBY SCHOOL

Books by Robert L. Guyer

Guide to State Legislative Lobbying (2000-2007, 3 editions)

Insiders Talk Series of Best Practices Manuals:
Manual 1. *How to Get and Keep Your First Lobbying Job* (2020)
Manual 2. *Glossary of Legislative Concepts and Representative Terms* (2019)
Manual 3. *How to Successfully Lobby State Legislatures: Guide to State Legislative Lobbying, 4th edition*—Revised, Updated and Expanded (2020)
Manual 4. *Winning with Lobbyists*, Readers edition (2019)
Manual 5. *Winning with Lobbyists*, Professional edition (2019)
Manual 6. *Guide to Executive Branch Agency Rulemaking* (2021, with Chris Micheli)

INSIDERS TALK: HOW TO GET AND KEEP YOUR FIRST LOBBYING JOB, Preparation, Potential Employers, and First-Day Performance

Copyright © 2020 Engineering THE LAW, Inc.
Published and Distributed by Engineering THE LAW, Inc.
www.lobbyschool.com

PRINT VERSION DATA
Requests for permission to make copies of any part of this book should be sent to:
Engineering THE LAW, Inc.
13714 N.W. 21 Lane
Gainesville, Florida 32606

Library of Congress Control Number: 2019917712
Main entry under title: Guide to State Legislative Lobbying
Print ISBN: 978-1-7323431-2-2
Ebook ISBN: 978-0-9677242-9-4

Book design by Sarah E. Holroyd (https://sleepingcatbooks.com)

This guide is dedicated to those wanting a fun, well-paying job helping others navigate government.

LOBBY SCHOOL

LOBBYIST CAREER DEVELOPMENT PLAN

YOU ARE HERE ⟹

Determine Candidate Lobbyist's Aptitude
Insiders Talk: How to Get and Keep Your First Lobbying Job

Suited to Lobbying — NO → **Do Not Lobby**

YES ↓

Overview Legislative Systems and Practice
Insiders Talk: Glossary of Legislative Concepts and Representative Terms

Grasp Concepts — NO →

YES ↓

Plan and Implement Legislative Lobbying Campaign
Insiders Talk: How to Successfully Lobby State Legislatures

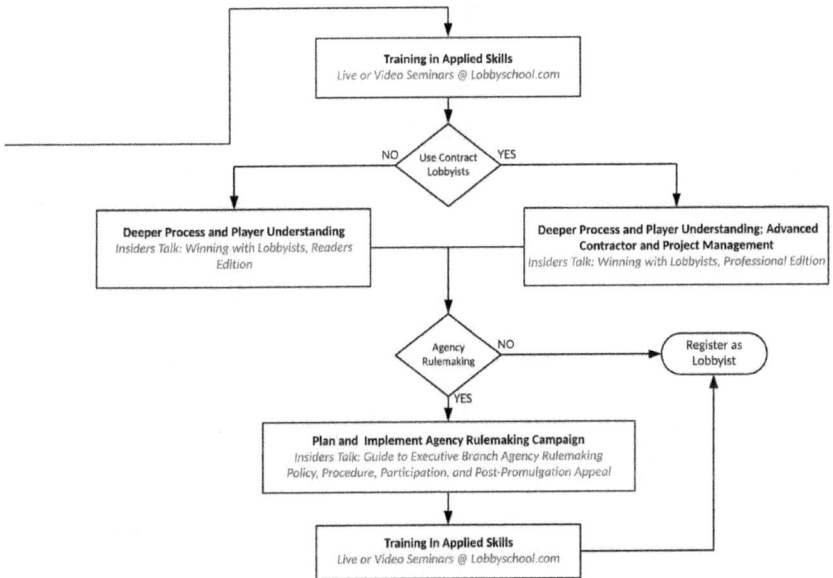

Training in Applied Skills
Live or Video Seminars @ Lobbyschool.com

NO ← **Use Contract Lobbyists** → YES

Deeper Process and Player Understanding
Insiders Talk: Winning with Lobbyists, Readers Edition

Deeper Process and Player Understanding; Advanced Contractor and Project Management
Insiders Talk: Winning with Lobbyists, Professional Edition

Agency Rulemaking — NO → **Register as Lobbyist**

YES

Plan and Implement Agency Rulemaking Campaign
Insiders Talk: Guide to Executive Branch Agency Rulemaking Policy, Procedure, Participation, and Post-Promulgation Appeal

Training In Applied Skills
Live or Video Seminars @ Lobbyschool.com

CONTENTS

FORWARD

I am fortunate to be a lobbyist in the State of California, working with amazing elected and appointed officials, their staff, and fellow lobbyists at our state's Capitol. After more than twenty years in this fulfilling profession, I still seek opportunities to gain knowledge and become a better lobbyist myself, and I spend a great deal of time passing along that knowledge to new lobbyists.

Robert Guyer and I share a passion for learning, for teaching, and for helping aspiring lobbyists to enter the profession we so enjoy. Robert has spent many years educating individuals about not only the "tricks of the trade" in order to be a successful lobbyist, but also the rationale for conducting ourselves in the way he describes in his seminars and his books.

When I first listened to his seminars, and then read his books, I kept saying to myself, "I agree! This is exactly what I tell people in the lobbying profession!" His experience at both the federal and state levels is unparalleled and the lobbying profession is fortunate to have him sharing his experiences.

This is his newest book in his *Insiders Talk* series and Robert tackles one of the most common questions that we both continue to get from those in the public and private sectors who want to join the lobbying ranks: "How do I get into your field?" Not only does Robert answer that important question, but also he helps you by explaining how to keep your job.

After reading this book, I am confident that you will have the necessary insights into pursuing a career as a lobbyist and that you will be prepared for succeeding in this profession that Robert and I cherish.

Chris Micheli
Aprea & Micheli, Inc.
Sacramento, California
October 2019

PREFACE

I am regularly asked, "How do I become a lobbyist?" A Google search of "How to become a lobbyist" produces about 6,790,000 results. A number of these basic overviews are useful.[1, 2, 3] This short book adds our take to answering that question plus two follow-up questions: 1) how get your first job and, 2) how to excel at it.[4]

My contribution to the answer comes from nine years participating in executive agency rulemaking, followed by nine years lobbying legislatures, and twenty years training lobbyists. During the eighteen years, I lobbied for corporations and industry associations in several U.S. states and in Washington, D.C.; for two years in Canada and before the Organisation for Economic Cooperation and Development (OECD) internationally; and for two years I assisted *pro bono* in enactment of Tennessee's *Long Term Community Choices Act of 2008*.

During twenty years training lobbyists, university lectures, and other public speaking engagements I have met thousands of new and aspiring lobbyists who want to know how to lobby, get a lobbying job, and how to excel in it. The *how to lobby* is answered by my live and video seminars and several *Insiders Talk* books. This book touches upon the how to get and excel in a job.

Lobbying can be a fun, well-paying, and interesting career in which you are always learning something new and dealing with interesting people. However, it isn't for everyone who thinks he or she may want to try doing it.

To help you decide if lobbying is for you, herein we go beyond basics of civics to discuss the realities of profession and prac-

3

tice, the great and the not so great. If after considering these realities you decide lobbying is really something you want to do, then we will examine your aptitude to be successful. That is, do you have what it takes to succeed? If you do, then we'll show you how to prepare for your first job, and discuss questions to consider with potential employers. We will finish with suggested actions to take on your first day of employment.

Working in an election campaign can be a great introduction to politics. Dr. Roger Austin and I in Appendix 1, *Can Working in an Election Campaign Help Me Achieve My Legislative Goals?*, discuss this avenue as a means for you to get to know process, lawmakers and their supporters and to build your own political influence. Relationships built and experience gained may make you a more attractive potential new hire.

Appendix 2, *Effective Lobbying Is Getting Votes, 27 Fundamentals for Successful Lobbying*, overviews the elements of effective lobbying. Study it as you consider a lobbying career. If you do become a lobbyist, read it each day to remind yourself of what lobbying really is and how to do it better.

ACKNOWLEDGEMENTS

None of my work is solely mine. I owe all my successes to those who have helped me to do better than I would have done on my own. Katherine Lee Amy Guyer, my beloved wife, is my inspiration, coach, and proofreader. Chris Micheli, principal Aprea & Micheli, Inc. (Sacramento), and author of hundreds of articles, proofread earlier drafts making key corrections and suggestions. Lobbyists from across the United States shared their anecdotes and observations. Some allowed attribution to their comments and others preferred to remain anonymous. To the anonymous as well as the identified, I say thanks and let's hope our collective wisdom benefits those who seek to enter lobbying.

INTRODUCTION

Lobbyists have a mystique about them of having money, influence, and power. As I explain below, a lobbyist's power is no more than the sum gravitas of his or her relationships. Like many professions, success is less about what you know than who you know. Section *Menu of Opportunities to Build Relationships*, the longest section of this book, will guide you in building those relationships.

Like most jobs, lobbying has its goods and bads, which we consider below. These include the dark side of being paid to win at all costs; having to tell your employer, that's not something the law allows, or you are willing to do; ethical conflicts among clients, lawmakers, and you making a good living; at times brutal working conditions; difficult people to navigate; and negative public perceptions of the profession.

Yet, it can be a great fit for those who care deeply about a cause, relish influencing people, enjoy interpersonal exchange, or just want an exciting and well-paying career. I loved being a lobbyist, as has virtually every lobbyist I've known over my 30 years in the field.

But in order to do well and to enjoy you work, you have to be suited for the job. You can initially estimate your suitability for the field by answering three basic questions:

- Do you know what lobbying is?
- Do you have the aptitude to succeed as a lobbyist?
- What kind of lobbyist would you like to become?

Over the next several sections we will examine these questions in detail. Your answers will help you determine if being a lobbying is something you really want to do. If it is, then we will guide you in getting your first job.

Do You Know What Lobbying Is?

Lobbying may be defined as, "trying to influence or gain good-will."[5] One seeks to influence and gain goodwill in order to sell. Selling is part of life and almost every successful person is a salesperson. In life you sell to your boss, your lover, and to anyone else who can give you what you want. Lobbying is selling laws.

However, unlike most sales activities, lobbying is highly regulated by law and by custom. The seller, less so the buyer, is the one who must beware in lobbying. It isn't *caveat emptor* (buyer beware) or even *caveat venditor* (seller beware), it's "deceive or lie to a lawmaker or staffer once and you are banned from the legislature, will be fired, are unemployable, and may face criminal, civil, or administrative sanctions."

Scrupulous honesty, I will regularly remind you, is at the foundation of a successful lobbying career. This leads us to discussing the first ingredient for an effective lobbyist, and, that is, being ethical.

Ethics. Except for a couple in D.C. and one or two at the state level, every lobbyist with whom I've worked has been of good to excellent moral character; and I would be proud to call most of them my friends. Lobbying lawmakers and staff is a trust-based profession. Senior lobbyist Rich Cranwell, says, "Lobbying is about connections, and building relationships. Trust is essential, and establishing this takes time and effort . . . to forge the relationships needed in today's political climate."[6] A lobbyist must have a reputation for integrity in order to thrive in this trust-based profession.

Trust rests upon the lobbyist's three top duties to lawmakers and staff: scrupulous honesty, accuracy, and credibility. Fifty sets of state ethics laws govern lobbyist-legislature interactions and etiquette governs the rest. The common purpose of formal ethics rules is to foster trust, civility, and honorable and legal behavior. Failure to remain ethical can cost a lobbyist trust, lobbying career, and professional, civil, and criminal penalties.

Some states regulate limited lobbyist-client behavior, such as Texas, where absent a waiver by both clients, a lobbyist may not represent clients with conflicting interests.[7] Few clients are sufficiently sophisticated to recognize, much less deal with, conflicts. Many hire contractors to avoid themselves having to deal with otherwise unpleasant task of having to protect their interests before government. I have written best practices manuals to produce and empower more sophisticated consumers of lobbying services, and lobbyists.

Trust is essential for having successful political, business and personal relationships. Cultivating a reputation of personal integrity leading to trust requires consistent good conduct among lobbyists and their clients. At a minimum, a long-term career requires conformity with legally and generally accepted ethics.

However, being ethical may be harder than that first sounds. Conflicts arise between principals and their lobbyists; between what principals want, on the one hand, and, on the other hand, what lobbyists want. For example, a client wants a favorable result, such as a tax benefit, and so does the lobbyist; but the lobbyist's body of rules limits how and what he or she can do to get results for the client.

9

Be warned that the lobbyist's duty of scrupulous honesty to lawmakers and staff flows in one direction and one direction only, that is, you to lawmakers and staff. It's not a reciprocal duty. Lawmakers, staff, other lobbyists, special interests, and the media will deceive you when expedient for them to do so. As a new lobbyist, the unscrupulous will try to compromise you for a momentary political advantage.

Ethical conflicts occur least when working as an in-house lobbyist, followed by being a contract lobbyist for honorable principals, and conflicts occur most when honest lobbyists work for win-at-all-cost clients. (I deal with a dishonest lobbyist working for a dishonest client below in *How to Prepare Yourself Before Starting Your Job Search*.) Let's consider this worst case first.

For win-at-any-cost clients, it's "I'm paying you to win, so do whatever it takes" – no excuses and few restraints. In part, this win-at-any-cost attitude may be why Americans rank lobbyists dead last among professions for honesty and ethics.[8] But a smart lobbyist always remembers that employers come and go but one's reputation is forever.

As you consider this field, you should be aware of the negative views many have for the lobbying profession, deserved for a few lobbyists but undeserved for the vast majority. Despite Gallup's public opinion poll[9] ranking lobbyists as almost as bad as Congress with low/very low ethics (58–60 percent), a long-term lobbying career is built upon scrupulous honesty, accuracy, and credibility.

Over my career, I've encountered disdainful responses upon revealing my profession. A lobbyist once told me that, when asked what he does for a living, rather than answer "lobbyist," he replies that he's a piano player in a D.C. brothel.[10]

Jimmy Williams' *Vox* article, "I was a lobbyist for more than 6 years. I quit. My conscience couldn't take it anymore," is written from the perspective of a "disgusted with the process" Washington, D.C. lobbyist.[11] While, I don't doubt Mr. Williams' experiences, but for the few scoundrels mentioned above, I never experienced or saw the things which he describes when I worked with lawmakers, either at the state or federal levels, as a client, or as an in-house or contract lobbyist. Colleagues polled for this paper agreed that honesty and integrity with lawmakers and staff are indispensable qualities for professional success and longevity.

If you can remain ethical and have the confidence and emotional strength to overcome occasional disapproval, then you have passed the first test. The next tests are: 1) to determine whether you can survive the working conditions; and, 2) to ask can you navigate the people with whom you will work.

Working conditions. Those who *call themselves* lobbyists fall into three broad categories: contract administrators, image representatives, and advocates. I will elaborate later on these groups but for now let's consider advocates, that is, *real lobbyists*.

For them, working hours *during the legislative session* are long. They start at early morning breakfasts and finish with after-dinner drinks. To outrival competitors, a one-state lobbyist has to keep these hours. The larger your geographic area of responsibility, the more you must travel the state, region, or nation and the more you must rely on assistance from contract lobbyists and associations. Itinerant lobbyists' hours are long because, in addition to lobbying, multistate lobbyists spend many hours in airplanes, hotels, and rental cars. After a few years, the mystique of travel and accumulating travel points wears off and it all gets very old.

For effective lobbyists, much of what takes place *during the session* stems from lobbying done *off-session*. *Off-session* the pace slows, but work remains constant building and fixing relationships with friends and foes, cultivating constituents, planning and preparing. Some lobbyists will be involved with executive agency rulemaking in which an agency could add more to what the legislature did, or take away much of what the legislature gave them.

If you conclude that you can stay ethical and handle the working conditions, then you are ready for perhaps the most difficult test. Can you can navigate the people with whom you will work?

Navigating the people. You will work with all kinds of people: the smart, the clever, the honorable, and a few not so much. Almost all of them are high-achievers sent to the capitol to advance special interests, theirs and their principals.

Nobody is sent to the capitol to be anyone else's friend, except to the degree situational acquaintances advance their principals' interests. This means you will have fake friends and seldom know who is real and who is not. Yet, per capitol etiquette and effective lobbying, you must deal with all of the special interests who can affect your bill, friend and foe. Talking to friendly people is easy. However, you also have to talk to people you don't like and who don't like you. To survive you must steel yourself to this unavoidable, forced unpleasantness.

You will deal with huge egos among lawmakers, special interests, staff, and lobbyists. At times their hubris is laughable, but it's also dangerous to you. Especially if you are young or new, some will attempt to tear you down to your face, in front of others, and behind your back. I lived those ambushes as a new lobbyist and saw it done to others.

12

Further most employers and clients expect you to be a true-believer, that is, a loyal member of their tribe *in good standing*. However, lobbyists have a legally enforced higher loyalty, that is, to abide by laws and etiquette of the legislature. For example, your marketing people may stretch the truth, to *puff*, in legal jargon. But if you are caught being *technically accurate but not entirely forthright*[12], then you no longer are going to be trusted in this trust profession. Without trust you are an ineffective lobbyist.

To be an effective lobbyist, you have to collaborate with organizations which, at other times and places, are your principal's competitors on appropriations, business, or policy. Your collaboration cannot be understood by many of your non-government affairs colleagues and you will have to navigate being seen by some of them as disloyal to your tribe.

Yet you must work with competitors in coalitions. Coalitions are filled with fair-weather friends, intrigue, and side-bar deals. Your partners are each doing their own cost-benefit analysis as to staying or quitting the coalition, and which coalition partners they will throw under the bus, if advantageous enough.

You will bear bullies who try to intimidate you and opponents who lie about you. You too will be tempted to mislead when you can close the deal with a word. Speaking to lobbyists about lawmakers, former U.S. House Speaker Tip O'Neill said, "Sometimes the members want you to tell them what they want to hear. Do not ever tell them what they want to hear; you always tell them what the right way is."[13] Scrupulously speaking the truth applies not only to lawmakers but also with everyone else with whom you work.

Don't play games. Be honorable with all. But be very cautious as to whom you trust. Any hint of your fakery, hypocrisy, or insincerity will undermine your career and aspirations. Be humble of heart with everyone, realizing you don't know everything and you have a lot to learn, and don't hit back. You'll lose. On the other hand, your grace under fire may earn you respect with some.

If you think you have passed all three tests, congratulations. Now let's examine whether you have the aptitude to be a lobbyist.

DO YOU HAVE THE APTITUDE TO SUCCEED AS A LOBBYIST?

"Aptitude: capability; ability; innate or acquired capacity for something; talent."[14] Some lobbyists have told me that lobbying can't be taught. "Indeed, many K Streeters [D.C. lobbyist district] simply believe the craft (and yes, it [lobbying] is considered a craft by many as well) is something you can't learn by reading a book. 'It's all about good instincts,' says Mike House, 'And instincts,' adds House . . .'can never be taught.'"[15]

Of course, I do not fully agree with Mr. House. I've taught thousands of people how to lobby. I knew immediately who wouldn't succeed; others were naturals. Some didn't have the ability, some refused to be taught, while some embraced the training and have excelled into important positions.

However, perhaps as Mr. House, I also recognize the innate, that is, the almost mystical ability to connect with another person enough to make the sale. But innate or acquired, everyone can increase their effectiveness from training. "There are always more tips and skills to learn about lobbying—it [the seminar] was great." Anita Farmer, Vice President, Georgia Government Affairs, Bank of America, Atlanta, Georgia.

There are degrees of lobbying proficiency. Those who have the aptitude do best, but others can be taught to do well. They have the above, "acquired capacity for something,"

The most important quality in a lobbyist is *personal integrity*. Liam Donovan, Director of Legislative Affairs, Associated Builders and Contractors, Inc., says, "Realize that your career has everything to do with your reputation. At the end of the day, your net worth is what people are saying about you. You need to develop all of these things: *smarts, hard work and integrity*."[16]

Can you persevere? Do you have a "steady persistence in a course of action, a purpose, a state, etc., especially in spite of difficulties, obstacles, or discouragement?"[17] Expect the most frequent response to your lobbying efforts to be "no." Your opponents are likely to be many. Some votes you will never get and some enemies are implacable. Can you bounce back from repeated "noes" and keep smiling, ready to try again?

For three years I travelled to Michigan, failing each year to enact a bill critical to my principal. Finally, in year three with the committee tied 2–2, the lawmaker with whom I had persevered most voted "yes." The committee favorably reported my bill 3–2 and that same session it became law.

For six years I lobbied in D.C. and year after year our team came up short. A change of party control in the Senate and unexpected fight between the House committee of jurisdiction and regulatory agency *lined up the stars* and the bill became law. We got our bill into law after six years. At that time, the rule of thumb for enactment was that from bill introduction to enactment took Congress about ten years, Congress having a ten percent enactment rate. The enactment rate is much lower today.

15

Can you live with failure? If you are trying to *enact* legislation, you will fail most of the time. To illustrate, for the first half of 2016, "19.3% of state Senate bills and 13.3% of state House bills are enacted on average compared with 3.6% and 1.9% of U.S. Senate and House bills respectively."[18] These are long-term trends.

Can you deal coolly within tense situations? During the committee hearing the Department of Natural Resources and its supporters were opposing my bill. Finally, the committee chair, wearied of them and me, said, "The committee is taking a 5-minute break. The Department, environmentalists, and industry are going to go into the hallway and bring us back a solution in 5-minutes." Under great pressure, we reached agreement. Can you?

Can you write? Clarity of thought and clear expression thereof are basic lobbying tools. Can you logically express concepts through words? Most lobbyists write frequently, at times under tense situations. They may have to be in the hallway drafting amendments, negotiating exact wording with supporters and opponents in the din of noisy crowds and intense pressure to get the amendment to its sponsor or legislative counsel before it's too late.

Do you have grace under fire? In lobbying you have to work with people you don't like and who don't like you. Can you do that? There are no "safe-spaces" in the capitol. Those whose views you don't like are not going to be "de-platformed." You have to argue against their views, and, ideally, get along with them outside the committee room. (You may need to become allies on a different issue.) A major-league Mid-Atlantic lobbyist comments, "This point can't be stressed enough, if you aren't the type of person who can have a conversation and meeting with people you don't like, and in fact may even politically detest, lobbying likely isn't the best career path to take."[19] This also means can you control your facial expressions and demeanor so as not to give away your position.

Are you likeable? People are predisposed to help people they like. They want to believe people they like. People are predisposed to go contrary to people they don't like.

Are you good at sales? Lobbyists are salespeople who know how to identify people's needs, connect with and cultivate them into customers, promise to meet their requirements, and eventually close the sale.

Do you have personal magnetism? This is physical attractiveness and personality. Attractive people do better in life. "There is a type of personality common among the best lobbyists, 'a certain undefinable quality that makes certain people appealing,' says one top Senate aide who has been lobbied hundreds of times over the course of a two-decade career."[20]

Are you attractive? Related to the preceding, a lobbyist's greatest asset is *attractiveness* because attractiveness leads to acceptance which leads to trust, which leads to sales. Attractiveness comes in many forms such as physical appearance and personality. "According to science, people who are perceived as attractive are more likely to get hired for jobs and seem trustworthy."[21] A female lobbyist once said to me, "I have been told by legislators many times, that [her looks] is how I got in their office, that is not how I got to stay in their office." Most lawmakers are 50+ year old males so her physical and emotional attractiveness opened doors for her.

Attractiveness also includes existing relationships, name recognition, and shared characteristics with those you want to influence. Shared characteristics are powerful motivators to being liked. As I emphasize in my books, *"The more you look like the customer, the more likely you'll make the sale."* This advice also applies to potential employers, clients, and lawmakers.

Notice I've said nothing about intelligence or education. While helpful, the ability to connect with another human being, especially one with power, trumps both. Smarts and education can be very important when lobbying executive agencies where facts and law rule. However, in the legislature, "Facts don't vote."[22] Who to believe and whom to support are more emotional responses rather than reasoned decisions.

The above qualities are advantages, just that, *advantages.* They do not define nor are they going to "make or break" your career. Whether you find a job or not depends on far more than just having the above pluses, as helpful as they are. Lobbyists come in both sexes, of all ages, shapes, sizes, colors, levels of attractiveness, ethnicities, political parties, body types, and educational levels.

Further, organizations tend to hire people who fit within their organizational mold, that is, who are like them. If you look like them and think like them, you have a better chance of getting a job. If you have the above, great; but if you don't, do not despair, you still have a chance. Now that you've decided that you would like to be a lobbyist and you have the aptitude, let's consider the job itself starting with the salary.

LOBBYISTS ARE PAID WELL

Whom you work for and where you work determine what you will be paid. Payscale.com reports $59,000 as the average U.S.

18

early career lobbyist annual salary, which scale ranges from $36,000 - $90,000 per year.[23] Public interest groups and small organizations pay less, while corporations and government pay are mid-range, and private lobbying firms set the top of the scale. City-specific annual early career salaries ranged from $51,000 in Harrisburg to $88,000 in Sacramento.

Salary.com, which provides state-by-state data, reports, "The average Lobbyist salary in the United States is $112,236 as of August 27, 2019, but the range typically falls between $90,480 and $154,710. Salary ranges can vary widely depending on many important factors, including education, certifications, additional skills, the number of years you have spent in your profession."[24] However, while the money is good, open jobs are few.

THERE AREN'T MANY *OPEN* LOBBYING JOBS

Lobbying is a hard field to break into and getting a job is an opportunity given to relatively few. An Internet job search will find few jobs advertised. Liam Donovan advises, "Doors open when they open. I would recommend sitting down with anyone you can, because this town [Washington, D.C.] is very fluid. It's about four things:

- Time
- Circumstances
- Luck
- Taking chances as they come."[25]

Finding a job is very much about being in the right place at the right time with some luck. You can increase your "luck" by doing the things discussed below.

Trends in employment. Part of the difficulty in finding employment is that lobbying does not employ many people. Today the number of registered state lobbyists is about the same as the number of floral designers (43,470), marriage therapists (42,880), and TSA officers (42,470). How many people do you know in these four professions?

The number of lobbyists has declined although the number of principals has increased. To illustrate, the National Conference of State Legislatures in 2006 reported in 34 states there were 44,430 registered state lobbyists; and, 40,152 principals.[26, 27] The *Lobby School* in 2016 tabulated from state websites 40,351 registered *state* lobbyists, and 54,159 principals in 35 states.[28] *Statista* reported in 2006 14,492 registered federal lobbyists and, in 2016, there were 11,182.[29] That is, from 2006 to 2016 the numbers of registered state and federal lobbyists decreased by ten percent and 23 percent, respectively. From 2010 to 2014 the numbers of federal principals decreased 25 percent.[30] However, from 2006 to 2016 the numbers of state lobbying principals increased 35 percent.

I have not researched an explanation as to why from 2006–2016 35 percent more principals became involved in state government affairs while the numbers of state registered lobbyists decreased ten percent. As for principals, I expect more are working in the states because, even if they have to do it state-by-state, they can get more done and faster than they can in Congress.

As to lobbyists, there are fewer in the states in part because of consolidation of organizations, the organizations that remain have been reducing the size of their government affairs staffs, and larger lobbying firms are buying up smaller firms. The result is fewer firms have more clients. Lobbyists, especially older ones, previously employed by the firms that went out of business are retired or are otherwise jobless. I know senior lobbyists who cannot find another job. Finally, some individuals lobby without registering or the thresholds triggering registration are so high that many lobbyists are not counted.

If after reading the above, you still want to pursue a lobbying career, I urge you to go ahead. The work is fun and pays well. You next have to choose what kind of lobbyist you would like to become. There are many kinds of lobbyists and lobbyist employers. You likely are better suited to one type and employer, rather than another.

WHAT KIND OF LOBBYIST DO YOU WANT TO BECOME?[31]

While lobbyist-employers include corporate, union, public interest, churches, professional, local and state government and other, lobbyists themselves fall into one of two groups, contract and in-house, as earlier noted. In-house lobbyists include administrators of lobbying contracts, image representatives, and advocates. By level of influence, a lobbyist falls into one of three categories: spectators, minor-leaguers, or major-leaguers.

Contract lobbyists sell advocacy services on the open market to any number of clients. This is the most demanding in terms of hours and stress but potentially it is the most financially profitable and topic-diverse form of lobbying.

An *in-house lobbyist* is an employee working for a single principal; often paid less than contractors but with less stress, more job security and, in most cases, better working hours.

- *Administrators of lobbying contracts* are primarily inter-faces between their principals and contract lobbyists. As contract administrators, they seldom go to capitols, much less lobby.

- *Image representatives* bring members of associations, unions, or public interest groups to capitols to make political statements, generally uncompromising. Appearance, not lawmaking, is their main purpose.

- *Advocates* lobby. They are in capitol hallways, work-ing with lawmakers and staff, negotiating with special interests, friends and foes.

Lobbyists have different levels of influence in the capitol.

- *Spectators* provide clients with information beyond that found in the capital's *Today in the Legislature* newslet-ter, attend public or coalition meetings on their clients' behalf, but have little influence in making laws.

- *Minor-leaguers* are often skilled, fully competent lob-byists but are limited in influence by lacking big-name clients or numbers of association members. As first noted above, a lobbyist is no more powerful than the sum gravitas of his or her clients or association mem-bers. Upon obtaining their first big-name principal, minor-leaguers move to the majors.

- *Major-leaguers*, while not necessarily more technically competent than minor-leaguers, have relationships with key lawmakers, a roster of big-name clients or association members, especially in-state, and campaign contributions that lead to considerable influence.

While other categories also exist, such as, registered lobbyists, non-registered advocates providing services just short of that legally defined as lobbying, and constituent-advocates, for our purposes, the above is a good start for discussion.

The question is less about which of the above do you want to be, but rather who gives you your first job, and that, in large part, depends on your relationships and luck. In my case, I was blessed with more than I could have dreamed with great employers, mostly decent professional colleagues, honorable issues for which to lobby, a good salary and great expense account.

MENU OF OPPORTUNITIES TO BUILD RELATIONSHIPS

Relationships are foundational to finding a job. "At least 70%, if not 80%, of jobs are not published," Matt Youngquist, president of Career Horizons told NPR. "And yet most people – they are spending 70% or 80% of their time surfing the net versus getting out there, talking to employers, taking some chances [and] realizing that the vast majority of hiring is friends and acquaintances hiring other trusted friends and acquaintances."[32]

To build relationships, I would advise someone wanting to go into lobbying, in order of opportunity for your professional development, to work with or as:

- Governor's office
- Legislator (capitol office)
- Legislator (district office)
- Non-partisan legislative office
- Executive agencies

- Public universities, hospitals, and quasi-public offices
- Local government
- Campaign worker or fundraiser
- Industry or professional association
- Association management company
- Corporations
- Public interest group or union
- Contract lobbying firm
- Law firm
- Lobbyist to executive agencies
- Local party executive committee
- Student government
- Graduate lobbying class
- Unpaid intern, volunteer, page, or fellow
- Other

While the discussion below focuses on *lobbying jobs* in the above categories, if you can't get the gold medal, then go for the silver or bronze. Just getting your foot in the door gives you exposure, relationships, and perhaps opportunity to shift to the position you really want. "For those individuals not currently employed in the Legislature or in the executive branch of state government, we have always strongly advised those individuals to get a staff position at the Legislature or in an administrative agency. This will enable you to develop an area of expertise in a policy area, to thoroughly understand the legislative process, and to develop working relationships with individuals inside and outside the State Capitol."[33]

For example, being a lawmaker's or committee's scheduler may not seem like the silver medal as you read this, but schedulers make face-to-face connections with potential employers, act on their requests for meetings, and dispense favors as when they move the requester to the much desired 9 a.m. time slot. They also exert power, as when saying, "I just can't fit your request in." And they benefit from knowing the capitol dynamic of people, process, and politics.

Choose carefully for whom you work because that job will define you for the next 10 to 20 years, if not your entire career. For example, if you work for the governor, every future mention of you will include, "former staff to Governor Smith." Work history pigeon holes you, opening or closing professional doors.

Governor's office. In-house lobbyists for the governor are lobbied by special interests thereby making important contacts. Further, like legislative staff, they deal with potential future employers from *their* staff positions of power, as discussed below. At the same time, they lobby legislators, legislative staffs, and special interests to support the governor's positions, so they are learning "how-to-lobby" skills. In many ways gubernatorial staffs receive the greatest education and foundation to become lobbyists because: 1) they learn how to be lobbied, as do legislative staff, *and*, 2) they also learn to lobby, like special interests do.

Other gubernatorial jobs can also open up opportunities to enter lobbying such as being a governor's press secretary, staff assistant, and similar positions. I have a colleague who was a governor's press secretary. Upon leaving the governor's office, she was hired to manage a large multistate government affairs office for a household-name organization.

Legislator (capitol office). Take a staff job in the legislature in whatever position you can find. To illustrate, "Most often, lobbyists get their positions because of their contacts and experience, with the vast majority having previously worked in California state government. Of course, there are many exceptions to this general rule."[34] In 2015, state legislatures employed 25,827 permanent staff and 5,547 session-only staff.[35] Once you have your foot in the door, then network to increasingly more important members, chamber leadership, and caucus – either party or issue-related. After you become permanent staff, your expected minimum time of service would be at least the term of the member you serve, two or four years.

In order of increasing job security and quality of relationships upon which you can build, from least to greatest, work for a freshman lawmaker, long-term lawmaker, leadership staff, committee staff, and most secure and desirable, party caucus staff. The more important your boss, the better your pay and the quality of contacts you will add to the current version of your digital Rolodex.[36]

After rank and file members, then working as personal staff for a committee chair is good, being committee staff is great, serving leadership is even better, and getting a job with the party caucus is the very best position for your lobbying future. In all you will learn how to wield your boss' power as you prepare for your own.

You will do this for either the majority or minority parties, wherever your politics lie. Be aware that party loyalty is the *sine qua non* when working for lawmakers. You are stuck with the politics you choose.

Staff, as everyone in the capitol knows, are extremely influential with members and committees. Because you as staff are in a power position, special interests will listen to you carefully, solicitously, and court your favor. They will read your every facial expression and inflection of voice. You have the chance to make a good impression from a power position – an on-the-job interview, of sorts – and also to discern organizations for which you might like to work.

But keep in mind legislative staff are governed by the same ethics laws as are lawmakers. You must never hint that you are looking for a lobbying job, nor show favoritism in hopes of building goodwill for future hiring. You are held to high ethical standards and liable for the consequences of violating ethics laws, rules, and etiquette. If you compromise your ethics it will become a topic of wide-spread gossip and your undoing.

On the other hand, you may try to become a lawmaker before becoming a lobbyist. While difficult, it is occasionally done.[37] As legislative staff, you can position yourself to assume your boss' job. In this case, work for a lawmaker, especially one who is likely to retire, run for higher office, become a lobbyist or association executive director, or be term-limited out of office. By working for the lawmaker, you will know the district intimately and build relationships with the lawmaker's supporters, voters, potential voters, donors, and players inside and outside the district, such as capitol special interest groups. Establish your domicile in the district and when the time comes, you will be poised to run. The gravitas of having been a lawmaker, knowledge of people and process, and professional courtesy lawmakers extend to each other are assets marketable to potential clients and employers.

If you become permanent staff for a committee that regulates industry, you could have a bright future ahead of you. You will develop detailed subject matter expertise, develop relationships with special interests, and connections with legislative and agency deciders, all of which are highly marketable. After five to ten years or so, you will work in the same environment, with the same subject matter, perhaps with the same committee staff, if not members, but move to the other side of the table as a highly paid lobbyist. A senior southern state lobbyist offers a different time line, "We are experiencing numbers of young people spending two to four years in service to a policymaker and jumping into the lobby arena."[38]

However, as to the solidness of the route, a Mid-Atlantic lobbyist affirms, "[T]he most frequent way I've witnessed others winning one of the coveted jobs is by being committee staff or state analyst. From nuclear to pharmacology, becoming an expert on the subject matter and the process opens many doors in the private sector."[39]

Watch out for your own hubris. If you are a good staffer, you can become your boss' alter-ego entrusted with doing most of his or her work and fully capable of replacing your lawmaker. Because staffs often control their members' votes, you are susceptible to seductions of power and self-importance. However, if you are perceived to be full of yourself, you will be unattractive to your member and potential employers.

Further, staffs, like lawmakers, know much about *being lobbied*, but initially they know little about *doing lobbying*. Their initial value isn't so much in doing lobbying as it is their knowledge of the legislative process, subject matter, players inside and outside the legislature, and *one-state* residual professional courtesy from former colleagues. So again, be humble, realize that you are at a good starting point but keep in mind you still have much to learn about designing a lobbying campaign, negotiating with special interests, client management, and the many other aspects of *doing lobbying*.

Finally, as a word of warning, former legislative staff upon becoming lobbyists may find it difficult to transition their loyalty away from the legislature over to their clients or employers. I advise clients and students not to too quickly trust former staff. I knew a newly hired senate staffer turned lobbyist who revealed her new employer's sensitive information to her friends still working in the legislature. She harmed her employer and lost her job and reputation. Wise employers carefully screen, instruct, and carefully monitor newly hired former staff to guard against betrayal, however unlikely.

Legislator (district office). While working in a lawmaker's district office offers considerably less capitol exposure, you nevertheless have your foot in the door with the lawmaker and get to know donors, party activists, and the all-important home-folk, that is, constituents. It also positions you to move to the capitol office or run for office later.

Non-partisan legislative office. These are the legislature's support services offices, for example sergeant at arms, bill room, or legislative services bureau. However, these are non-political jobs and any hint of your being party biased would harm the image of the office and your career. Nevertheless, you can get to know lawmakers and special interests through them, and establish yourself as a policy and procedure expert.

Executive agencies. You can lobby the legislature on behalf of an executive agency. Often the job title is *government relations, legislative affairs, legislative services, intergovernmental relations* but most generically simply *legislative liaison*. Special interests, supporters and opponents, negotiate with agency staff because an agency's support or opposition to their legislation often is the deciding factor in a bill becoming law. The legislative liaison in turn works with them to support or not oppose department legislation. Agency legislative liaisons build relationships with lawmakers, staff, and special interests, including potential employers. They learn negotiation and legislative procedure, develop subject matter expertise, and persuasion skills. They also participate, at least informally, in coalitions.

However, as in the legislature, an agency's legislative liaison can have one of three roles: spectator, analyst, or advocate. *Spectators* observe the legislature's committees; and, their presence in committee rooms communicates agency interest in what lawmakers are doing.

Analysts provide fact-and-law unbiased technical advice to lawmakers. Getting partisan, that is going beyond that which aids agency compliance with its enabling legislation, could undermine agency (and your) reputation for unbiased information on which the agency and your own credibility rest *with both political parties*. While agency staff may present policy positions of agency management, taking political sides could cause incalculable harm to both the agency and to your future work as a lobbyist.

Advocates are analysts who additionally work with other special interests, especially government agencies, to advance agency positions, particularly appropriations. They foster *non-political party* mutual interest alliances. For example, the department through the liaison may work with a public employees' union to increase the numbers of prison guards in order to improve prison safety for both the incarcerated and corrections officers. The payback for the union is more public employees to join the union.

He or she might collaborate with another government department on a bill affecting both agencies. Or he or she could collaborate with municipal governments on matters of overlapping concern such as environmental protection.

Special interests may lobby the legislative liaison in order to get him or her to intervene with agency political appointees to redirect or shut down agency legislation or rulemaking. Special interests have to demonstrate to the liaison that a proposed agency action will, over the long term, harm the agency before the legislature. The advocate thereby additionally gains coalition and negotiating experience.

You can also participate in rulemaking, which is agency development of administrative law to implement statutory law. While you won't work with legislators, in rulemaking you get to know many of the same organizations that lobby the legislature and you will develop subject matter expertise. On the other hand, legislative staff may contact you when technical questions arise about a bill the legislature is considering.

If you bring agency trust and respect, your greater value to a potential employer may be that of an agency lobbyist representing your principal, as mentioned below. However, that same trust would be useful to you working with the legislature. So you would offer a potential employer influence first with the agency and secondly with the legislature, a unique combination that could be marketable.

Public universities, hospitals, and quasi-public offices. Public institutions hire contract lobbyists or use their own in-house lobbyists, often both. These lobbyists carry the gravitas of representing divisions of state government, large and widely-known institutions, subject matter expertise, and often serving many citizens in multiple legislative districts.

Local governments. Local governments spend considerable time and money lobbying state and federal governments. "In many states, local governments spend more on lobbyists than both business and unions."[40] Local governments lobby in state capitols as members of associations and as individual entities. State associations include states' leagues of cities, municipal leagues, associations of counties and boroughs.

Local governments hire contract lobbyists and use their staff to lobby.[41] Large local governments have internal offices of government affairs.[42] Others have staff working full-time or part-time as lobbyists, often working from the city or county managers' offices. School boards lobby, as do tribal governments.

Campaign Worker or Fundraiser. Working with lawmakers in their electoral campaigns lets you develop relationships with select lawmakers and their supporters, especially donors. Dr. Roger Austin and I discuss this in Appendix 1, *Can Working in an Election Campaign Help Me Achieve My Legislative Goals?* Working in a campaign provides short-term exposure to one or more lawmakers or candidates who may prove useful to your career.

A fundraiser meets the principal donors who finance lawmakers' election campaigns and to whom lawmakers are indebted for financial support. By being known as a person who can raise money, lawmaker gratitude that comes with receiving money, and the connections you make with donors, you develop marketable relationships.

Industry or professional association. Associations offer two avenues for becoming a lobbyist. The first is to work in the association's government affairs department as an in-house lobbyist or non-lobbyist government affairs manager. The second is to position yourself to be hired by an association member as their in-house lobbyist or staff in its government affairs department.

An association *non-lobbyist* government affairs manager is essentially an administrator of lobbying contracts, mentioned above. Associations can have single-state, regional, or national interests. These managers are their employers' interfaces with one to dozens of lobbyists across the United States, each lobbyist having varying levels of work. This can be a full-time management position.

This manager works remotely compiling information supplied by association or contract lobbyists to apprise its association government affairs department, management, or association legislative committee. He or she may relay policy direction to contractors; this manager is seldom, if ever, in state capitols or lobbying.

Association *in-house government affairs staff* lobbies to the degree resources of personnel, time, and money permit. An association interested in one-state lobbying can fully participate in the capitol. As geographical areas of responsibility increase, resource-deficient lobbyists hire contractors. In time they come to resemble non-lobbyist government affairs managers but also may lobby putting out legislative fires. This lobbyist faces burnout as described below in section *How to Prepare Yourself Before Starting Your Job Search*, subsection "Are you strong enough to avoid burnout?"

Positioning yourself to be hired by an association member is another way to get a lobbying job. The more important the association and the greater its members in numbers and wealth, then the greater the opportunity you will have to serve the association and to showcase yourself and your talents to potential employers. I have seen young association staff parlay association employment into plum corporate jobs. Try to work directly in the association's lobbying arm, as staff to the executive or legislative committee, or executive director. As you grow in expertise in the association's mission, knowledge of its issues and members you become more valuable to all. Position yourself to be your association's representative or backup to the state's Society of Association Executives.

Industry associations often have the greatest insight into jobs available with their members. For example, as of this writing the 350-member Washington Area State Relations Group, which bills itself as " . . . one of the nation's largest organizations dedicated exclusively to serving state government relations professionals," lists seven lower level jobs. On the other hand, in California,

> More often than not, potential employers looking for a lobbyist will advertise for the position. There are open job listings that are regularly posted on the websites of *Capitol Morning Report, Capitol Weekly, The Nooner,* and *Capitol Daybook.* These days, almost every open lobbying job can be found in these job postings. It is important to look at these each and every day. Some jobs are posted for several weeks, while others may be there for just a few days.[43]

The Public Affairs Council lists several jobs, primarily in the Washington, D.C. area but some in the states.[44]

Association management company. Smaller associations often are managed by association management firms. "They offer the expertise, staffing and resources that allow professional societies, trade groups, not-for-profits and philanthropic organizations to effectively manage day-to-day operations and advance their long-term goals."[45] They may manage the state lobbyists' association and offer government affairs representation and advice to their clients.

Corporations. These are the fountains of money, expertise, and power first in influence in most state capitals and Congress. Lawmakers are almost exclusively motivated by the special interests that put them in power and keep them there. Corporations are a major segment among special interests.

However, most, but not all, in-house government affairs offices run lean on *in-house* personnel. When I worked for Ralston Purina, now Nestlé Purina and still one of the largest corporations in America, we had two federal lobbyists and one state lobbyist (me). Corporations prefer to hire *contract lobbyists* who can easily be terminated, unilaterally have their compensation reduced, and be reassigned, at least in C-suite theory. I observed this in almost all of the hundreds of corporations with which I interfaced.

As of this writing, for example, in Washington, D.C. Facebook[46] and Apple have 8-person offices, Google 13, and Amazon recently went from 14 to 28.[47] However, these companies are represented by hundreds of lobbyists throughout the country, not only in large states like California and New York but also in smaller states like Idaho and South Dakota. Of course, they also have teams of in-house managers directing their contractors.

Sales can be another indirect avenue into corporate government affairs. I have known several former salespeople move within their corporations from product sales to government affairs and do quite well. It's just selling a different kind of product for the same employer.

Public interest group or union. Having had these groups as clients and *Lobby School* participants, often they are more ideological representatives than lobbyists. That is, "If the choice is between securing and keeping votes and projecting their organization's dogma, they choose dogma. The idea politics is the art of compromise is anathema because compromise is beneath them."[48] In states in which they are powerful, association with them may not harm you. However, working for them may limit your future opportunities by pigeonholing you in the public sector niche.

Contract lobbying firm. The hours are long, client demands at times exhausting, conflicts of interest abound, and the rewards very high with the right firm. There are thousands of contract lobbying firms in the United States ranging from one person working out of his or her home office (Oklahoma) to silk-stocking[49] firms with dozens of employees (New York, California, Florida). However, most lobbying firms are smaller organizations. You get to know their clients and other lobbying firms as potential employers. If you leave to form your own firm some of their clients may want to move with you.

Law firm. Law firms offering contract lobbying services and, as profit making entities, share many of the characteristics of contract lobbying firms. However, law firms' expectations of their associates go beyond the long hours of the legislative session. The constant firm demand on associates as to both working and billable hours can be brutal. "Fifty-seven percent of lawyers who were working at the largest firms two years into their careers (2002) had moved on by 2007."[50] This number is consistent to what I heard even back when I was in law school, and that is, fifty percent of lawyers quit the practice of law within seven years of graduation.

Non-lawyers working as lobbyists in law firms have told me lawyers see non-lawyers as second-class citizens for lacking a Juris Doctor degree and a bar number. They just aren't part of the fraternity. In time the class distinction of inferiority takes an emotional toll upon the non-attorney lobbyist. *Res ipsa loquitur* ("*the matter speaks for itself*"), as lawyers say.

Lobbyist to executive agencies. Similar to being a lobbyist *for an executive agency* above, you can also be a lobbyist *to an executive agency.* Your agency work develops deep technical knowledge, understanding of both legislative and administrative law, adeptness at technical argument, and you make valuable contacts. Most principals involved in legislative lobbying are also involved in executive agency lobbying, especially through the rulemaking process. Your state may require you to register as an executive agency lobbyist.

Local party executive committee. As a former party executive committee member, I saw party executive committees largely populated by successful older people having relationships with local, state, and, occasionally, federal office holders. We welcomed young people in part because, being young, they are by definition *the future.* We found hope for the party's future in their youth, enthusiasm, and willingness to work. And helping the local party can foster relationships with the state party, maybe a job, and more exposure to potential employers.

Student government. Student government is a good place to get to know future state leaders. Two very successful young lobbyists I know were big in student government; one just made partner in a major lobbying firm after only four years employed. I have no personal experience with student government, so I will say little more about it.

Graduate lobbying class. Universities valuing applicable knowledge may offer graduate lobbying classes. Students often are working professionals, especially working in state government and the legislature, and lobbyists wanting to advance their careers by getting a master's degree. I taught the course *Lobbying* in Florida State University's *Masters of Applied American Politics and Policy* and found highly motivated mature students. Relationships made and skills learned could serve a lobbyist well. However, do not overestimate the value of the degree itself *for getting a job.* T.R. Goldman writes,

> [I]t might get you no more than a very expensive piece of paper, one that costs $1,500 for a certificate of completion for American's [American University] course and as much as $47,160 for the 36 credit-hours it takes to earn a full-blown master's of political management at George Washington. It certainly won't let you waltz into one of the city's thousands of lobby shops with a guaranteed position—particularly not in today's tight job market.[51]

However, beyond simply just holding another degree, getting the right education from the right people can help you. The right people are a faculty, full or part-time, consisting of current and former legislative affairs practitioners. Adjuncts especially know the legislative players - lawmakers, staff, and special interests - and trends in the state house. And such faculty can make introductions for you, advise you on your job search, and help you once employed.

Study applicable technical courses such as bill drafting and legislative procedure. I have found few lobbyists understand legislative procedure although infrequently that knowledge is literally indispensable to achieving client satisfaction. Holding yourself out as a specialist, especially in a technical arena such as legislative procedure and bill drafting, should make you stand out among your competitors.

Unpaid intern, volunteer, page, and fellow. The ad reads, "The organization is hiring a Political Affairs Intern who will meet directly with Congressional offices in their region and be part of all aspects of building support for life-saving legislation. This is a part-time, 14-hour per week, unpaid internship working remotely. College credit is available."[52] The Congressional Research Service[53] makes clear distinctions among interns, volunteers, fellows, or pages. I have no experience with these opportunities; however, for sake of completeness, I list them without comment.

Other. Your goal is to build relationships with lawmakers, lobbyists, and potential employers regardless of wherever they are. For example, lawmakers and lobbyists frequent a limited number of bars and restaurants. You can engage them by working in one and maybe even overhear gossip. Learn from bartenders at high volume establishments who excel in connecting with a customer in ten seconds, almost regardless of customer. The really serious ones prepare themselves to connect to anyone, in part by reading the headlines of the day to make themselves ready to be "all things to all people."

Clyde's and Costello's in Tallahassee is such a place and when liquor is involved, one can learn much and begin *cautiously and subtly* cultivating relationships. A Republican operative emailed me, "I have also heard . . . that some organizations use what I refer to as 'horizontal lobbyists.' And this is partially for ingratiation, perhaps gentle persuasion later, etc. It's all very low key and subtle."

However, you must be honorable and respected by all and likeable by most. Any hint of fakery, hypocrisy, insincerity, or *job hunting on their time*, will be found out and your career and aspirations undermined.

In my case, I interviewed for a job with a major company that I did not get. However, they shortly thereafter found themselves unexpectedly needing a lobbyist and remembered me. I had made a good impression. I interviewed for their lobbying job, got it, and had a great career, leading to state, federal, and international lobbying. You just never know what connections will help you in unexpected times. So make a good impression wherever you go.

You Have to Be Good, but Being Good Isn't Necessarily *Good Enough*

Some years ago I went to open mic night at the Bluebird Café in Nashville. Four performers sat side-by-side taking turns sharing their music. The first completed her song and I thought to myself, "This woman is fantastic. Why isn't she famous?" And with each successive musician, I observed the same high quality and asked the same question. The last performer sang about two old dogs in his front yard with such tenderness that he brought me misty eyes. And again, I asked, "Why isn't he famous?" The answer is in getting a job, like in making music, being good isn't necessarily good enough.

Excellence is only the first step. Tens of thousands of excellent people want to be lobbyists, or musicians who can earn a living. But, as Liam Donovan said above, getting a lobbying job is about time, circumstance, luck, and taking chances as they come. Just like making it in music.

You may get a job working as staff, serve long term in the legislature, and have a successful position with a corporation or other employer. However, that doesn't mean you will find employment afterwards. And I get calls from top level lobbyists who, upon being laid off, never find their next government affairs jobs.

For this paper, I spoke directly with a former legislative staffer and now government affairs director for a national association; a corporate lobbyist; and a former lawmaker. The staffer turned government affairs director moved from D.C. to Florida, but hadn't found work in Florida, as of this writing. The corporate lobbyist, also having moved from D.C. to Florida, after years of looking hasn't found an employer there despite having extensive experience in energy and utilities. The lawmaker with decades in the legislature couldn't find work because he had no clients to bring to lobbying firms.

Thankfully, their fates are not so bleak. The former lawmaker and corporate lobbyist work for themselves. The former lawmaker eventually built a successful 16-client solo lobbying practice in the state capital. For any contract lobbyist, getting the first client is the hardest thing to do. You can't get the next client until you get the first. He finally got that first client and built from there.

The corporate lobbyist's former employer considers him so valuable as to keep him working part-time remotely. The same occurred with the staffer turned government affairs manager. When I was laid off in a corporate takeover, a former boss hired me to run his government affairs program, although 2 years later I lost that job in another corporate takeover of that same employer.

So while you are employed, build all your credentials and deepen relationships as much as you can. While you have a job, always be preparing yourself to lose it and be ready to strike out on your own. Keep good relationships with potential clients and everyone else, as you can.

Whether you find an employer or end up working for yourself, you will have a better career by first thinking through who you want to be as a lobbyist. Then upon landing a job, by knowing what needs to be done immediately upon employment, you will steer your future. You begin by preparing yourself.

How to Prepare Yourself *Before* Starting Your Job Search

Let's consider some questions that should be settled *before* you look for a job. Your answers set the foundation for your professional future, success, job satisfaction, and longevity. Those of you already employed must consider these same success-defining foundational questions.

- What do you bring to a potential employer?
- Who do you want to be in your organization?
- Are you strong enough to avoid burnout?
- How government affairs sophisticated is your employer?
- How committed is your employer to an effective government affairs program?
- How committed is your employer to you?
- Can you do well in a logical but often wholly irrational environment?
- Can you make sound decisions under great pressure?
- Are you prepared to protect your integrity and your dignity?

What do you bring to a potential employer? At this point we take it that you have the aptitude to be a lobbyist. So what makes you so unique that an employer would want to hire you among the talented hundreds looking for a job? In most lobbying circumstances, the employer pretty much holds all the cards because good hires are everywhere and jobs are few. You must be confident in what you offer.

"It's not what you know; it's who you know," goes the old saying. So who do you already know in the legislature, local politics, party leaders, and donors? Have you volunteered in a political campaign and gotten on a first name basis with the candidate, now hopefully a lawmaker, and with those who supported him or her, especially donors?

Do you have a recognizable name? Were you a local sports star, for example? I know a young man who got a national hockey championship ring for his university winning the national hockey crown. That ring and a career in professional hockey made him an ideal hire in his state. Although he chose to sell stocks rather than sell laws, he could have easily gotten a job doing either. Be ready to clearly state what makes you unique among the many. So what does?

Who do you want to be in your organization? Your first step to finding your "place" is to define your "self," that is, who you want to be and how you want people to see you. Settle this in your own mind *before* the interview. Think of yourself, regardless of organization size or your age, as being in the *C-Suite*, even if your future employer doesn't have one, as such. This may require effort on your part.

As a caution for females, over many years I have observed a female tendency of lower job-status women trying to make a higher status female new-hire "one of the girls." Beyond collegiality and friendliness, they do this in order to share the new hire's power and simultaneously diminish the status gap between her and them. The net result can be a reduction in her organizational gravitas which will carry over to her sense of self and presence in the capitol. She must keep firmly in mind that she is her organization's face to the legislature, influencing and meeting with lawmakers, negotiating bills with powerful special interests, and in a real sense holding her organization's wellbeing in her hands. Of course, be professional with everyone in the office but, in your position, you cannot let yourself be "just one of the girls."

Male or female, you will be known by the company you keep and the professional image you project. Act and dress like who you want to be in five years. This prepares you and your management for that moment and, in the meanwhile, you will do better in the office, with your colleagues, and with the legislature.

Create or change your online persona because potential employers will search for your social media presence. "According to a 2018 CareerBuilder survey, 70 percent of employers use social media to screen candidates during the hiring process, and about 43 percent of employers use social media to check on current employees."[54] Scrub controversial posts – Facebook, Instagram, Twitter, Snapchat or whatever is in vogue when you read this. Start a blog that reflects who you want to be perceived as, which may not be as you have portrayed yourself in the past. Put up YouTube videos showing to the world your preferred image.

If you apply to a larger organization, expect either their Human Resources department or a contactor such as HireRight to do a background check in which they will find out everything about you, good and ill. A controversial social media history can harm you greatly. Clean it up and create a new persona. Some companies offer fee-based services to clean up online reputations.

Are you strong enough to escape burnout? Will you be the only government affairs professional or one of many? Most, but not all, organizations are lean on in-house government affairs staff. If it looks like you will be worked to death for lack of depth in your organization or lack of contractor support, think twice if this is what you want to do, for how long, and if this is the right employer for you.

How long was your predecessor on the job? Why did he or she leave? Was it because of job burnout? I was once hired because the person currently in the job was exhausted. I took the job not really knowing the toll extensive travel takes. For six grueling years, I was in the top one percent of the top one percent of Delta Air Line's frequent fliers. And I was flying other carriers, too! Expect to do this if you get into multistate lobbying.

If you work for a one-state profit-making company or an association thereof, during a session you may be expected to work the same long hours as contract lobbyists do – start at 6 a.m. and home by 11 p.m. Such expectations are seldom the case for grant-funded or dues supported membership organizations. Will your employer make time for an end-of-session rest period?

If your new employer wants you to be a *real lobbyist*, that is, doing advocacy, then you will be traveling the state off-session for meetings with lawmakers and potential political supporters and opponents. In either case, determine beforehand how much travel you are willing to do. Their travel expectations can be estimated by the travel budget they have for the position. If it's anemic, you may find yourself assigned to other duties rather than being a full-time lobbyist. I tell lobbyists that if they are in their offices for more than three days a week off-session they probably are not doing the job they were hired to do.

45

How government affairs sophisticated is your employer? Especially in corporate America, employees are hired to produce results for organizations competing in the marketplace. For profit-making companies, this means vanquishing enemies, that is, business competitors. At the same time, legislators expect consensus among similarly situated groups; and, if they don't see it, then they become wary about getting involved in "turf wars." Because interest group coalitions are foundational politically and tactically, you are going to collaborate with marketplace competitors in a, "We must, indeed, all hang together, or most assuredly we shall all hang separately."[55]

However, unsophisticated fellow employees may see you "fraternizing with the enemy." I once had a VP tell me I was making the "wrong kinds of friends" to the distress of his marketing team. However, to top management, I was getting the laws they needed to stay in business. Nevertheless, unaware employees may doubt your loyalty and you may find yourself disconnected from the tribe.

Further, unsophisticated management may think you an unproductive employee because you did not meet your annual goals, such as enacting a specific law. All company employees have on-time deliverables. Manufacturing did it; marketing did it; how come you didn't get the bill repealed? Many don't grasp that the legislature often is a wholly irrational body. They are politicians, act and think like politicians, which utterly befuddles the C-Suiters who ask, "Why doesn't government operate like a business?"

How committed is your employer to an effective government affairs program? Lobby School students, especially those working for tax-supported, grant-funded, or membership-based organizations, have told me that they thought they were being hired to be lobbyists only to find themselves also working as part-time meeting planners, membership marketers, and helping out with database management. An uncommitted employer may want a warm "jack of all trades" body, not an effective lobbyist. You can find yourself with a title of Government Affairs Manager, but in reality, your employer is not committed to government advocacy during the off-session when you should be planning and building for next session.

Sometimes this is because the above kinds of organizations only want earlier discussed *administrators of lobbying contracts* and *image representatives* rather than advocates. Administrators of contracts can work for any kind of organization. Image representatives show the organization's colors, make political statements, and bring members to the capitol. Advocates, on the other hand, focus on getting legislative results, which leaves little time for non-lobbying tasks.

How committed is your employer to you? You can estimate just how committed the employer is to you by asking your management to make clear to the association's contract lobbyist that he or she is there *to support you.* I've seen contractors marginalize new hires in order to keep control of the client's government affairs program. At times contractors ally with management, especially in membership associations, to protect each other to the detriment of the association and its nominal leadership. Without strong support and direction from management, you may find yourself in conflict with both contractor and your boss, leading to a short unhappy career.

Your employer's government affairs sophistication and commitment to you will greatly affect your longevity and happiness on the job. Working for a sophisticated employer which is committed to its government affairs program and to you will be a tremendous experience.

47

Can you do well in the logical but often wholly irrational legislative environment? Lobbying is logical in that it follows a series of predetermined, formal, sequential, written, and mandated steps, such as those found in the state constitution, statutes, and chamber parliamentary procedure. The predictability and transparency of the *formal processes* are why you can plan and implement a structured and step-by-step lobbying campaign. That is, everybody starts at step A and finishes at step Z, and it's all laid out on a state-published flow chart.

However, simultaneous with and parallel to the formal processes are the *informal processes*. These are often characterized by the petty, arbitrary, capricious, unpredictable, at times unseemly, and often laughingly nonsensical. The informal but often seemingly irrational processes are called *politics*.

To be successful you have to navigate both. But are you willing to? I recently spoke to a state organization attempting to organize its 10,000 members into a grassroots lobbying force. After my presentation, one listener came up to me to say that he expects lawmakers to behave "more professionally" than I had described. I took "more professionally" to mean he expects lawmakers to rise above the politics into which he refuses to descend and in which politicians exist.

Irrationality, divorced from facts and public policy, all too often characterizes the legislative process. Before you become a lobbyist you have to answer for yourself, "Can I do well in a logical but often wholly irrational environment?" Each day you go into the office ground yourself by rereading Appendix 2, *Effective Lobbying Is Getting Votes! 27 Fundamentals for Effective Lobbying*.

Can you make sound decisions under great pressure? Representing your principal can be pressure-filled, especially when immediate on-the-spot decisions are demanded. Occasionally an ineffective client forces a contractor to make decisions belonging to the client alone. However, for an in-house lobbyist, who is both client and lobbyist in the same person, the pressure is inescapable. Expect one day, just prior to the committee vote the chair will look up to ask you directly, "Can (your principal's name) live with this?" It's now or never for your decision. Fail to answer and the process goes forward without you. I have faced committing my entire industry to millions of dollars of costs in that one split-second answer and so will you. Can you do that?

Are you resolved to protect your integrity and your dignity? Superseding a principal's short-term interests, we lobbyists have a higher duty and that is to safeguard the integrity of the legislature, the public's respect for how laws governing them are made and, of course, our profession and reputation.

And to protect the institution, lobbyists caught lying to the legislature will find their careers over and even face criminal charges. A committee chair once said to a group of us about a lobbyist we all knew, "He lied to us once. He'll lie to us again. And he'd better never show his face again before the Senate Natural Resources Committee." This lobbyist's career was over until everyone who knew of his lying had been term-limited out of office.

Further, when caught lying, your principal to save its capitol influence will have to fire you as a "rogue employee,"[56] doubly ending your lobbying career. You are now known as a liar who was fired from your job for dishonesty. Not only is your lobbying career over, but also future unrelated job opportunities. A senior lobbyist advises, "Never compromise your long term career for a short term gain for your current employer. Your employer is likely to change, multiple times, during your career as a lobbyist. However, your reputation follows you throughout. You can't live to fight another day if you have a career ending ethical lapse."

On the other hand, while you may lose a dishonest principal, your reputation for integrity may help you in the future. I was laid off in a corporate downsizing (a lobbyist is just overhead!) and immediately my former supervisor who had become an association executive unexpectedly called me up for a two-year international lobbying gig. He needed honest talent and sadly had been ripped off by a contractor with neither.

A powerful D.C. lobbyist once said to me, "Lobbying is a dance of seduction," and often, as noted above, lawmaking is unrelated to facts and good public policy. There are other motivators at work. And while he didn't mean seduction in a salacious way, the unseemly connotation cannot be ignored. Lawmakers have to be motivated to buy your legislative position rather than selecting your opponent's. While almost always motivated by the legal, sometimes lawmakers are less than sterling in their own characters. Lawmakers may exploit lobbyists and their principals, as lobbyists and their principals exploit lawmakers.

Lawmakers can exploit lobbyists and their principals because the lobbyist-lawmaker power-balance often tilts very much in the lawmaker's favor. They can vote for or against you and, except at election time, they are largely unaccountable for what motivates them to vote one way or another. I won't go into detail of some scandalous motivators; the media report enough of them and the Internet is littered with their destroyed reputations. But know this, if you accede to unseemly motivators, legal or not, it will not remain secret. Exposed, you will be held in lower esteem damaging, if not ending, your career.

You must protect your dignity, as well. Some will try to get you to do things you will regret later. A *Lobby School* participant, the son of a former governor told his class, "My dad and I were at church in line waiting to go to communion. A lobbyist came up to my dad and put his business card into his hands. My dad ripped up the business card on the spot." That lobbyist's lack of dignity is now is in his state's lobbying lore. Others will exploit especially the young relying on the old truism, "The strength of the young is no match for the treachery of the old." Behave as the person you would like to be known as.

Never compromise your integrity or your dignity. Don't allow yourself to seduce or to be seduced. The temptations will be there. But wrongly behaving could cost you your career and job future. *Insiders Talk: Winning with Lobbyists, Professional edition* Chapter 12, "Power and Corruption" and Chapter 13, "Ethics Laws for Lobbyists and Clients" provide much ethics advice as to how to protect your professional career.

The job interview. Keep firmly in mind that you are interviewing, intentionally or not, during every interaction with lawmakers, staff lobbyists, association executives and other potential employers and clients. Many useful general guides for interviewing are easily found on the Internet. For a lobbying interview, I would add four rules:

- Let your face be seen.
- Likeability is job #1.
- Know your customer.
- Customers buy to meet their needs, not yours.

Let your face be seen. Be at committees considering for your bill, in the hallways, at the fundraisers, drop by their offices off-session and unobtrusively during session. Make sure lawmakers, staff, friends, and foes know you are there. All will be more honest knowing you might catch them sabatoging your bill. You build awareness, familiarity, and relationships, and you lobby just by being in their field of view, background or foreground.

Likeability is job #1. If they like you, they might listen to you and, if they listen to you, they might be willing to do what you want. If they don't like you, they at best won't hear a word you say and at worst they will seek to avoid or even harm you. Foundational to being likeable is sincerity, confidence, and humility. Charles Spurgeon observed, "The imitation of humility is sickening; the reality is attractive." As I discuss below, lots of incompetent people have successful careers just because they are likeable.

Know your customer. In lobbying this means you know the candidate-employer, staff, the employer's clients, campaign contributions, and issues lobbied. Much of these data are readily available, especially on state websites. It lets you know if you would want to be associated with the firm and, if you do, enable you to converse insightfully with them about issues in which they are interested. You must compile a dossier on each potential employer.

Customers buy to meet their needs, not yours. Employees are hired to the degree they assist an employer to satisfy its needs. Interview with the attitude, "I'm here to help you meet your needs and I have the capacity to do it." More bluntly, nobody really cares what your needs are except to the degree the employer can satisfy those needs in order to get and keep a productive employee and not waste the time and money hiring someone who won't work out.

WHAT TO DO ON YOUR FIRST DAY ON THE JOB

Congratulations, you're hired! This section provides career defining steps for *newly hired* lobbyists, advising you to:

- Read *70 Experts Share Their Best Advocacy Planning, Strategy, Skills and Training Tips,* by Ann Dermody.[57]
- Bolster yourself with formal training and supplemental resources.
- Learn your employer's political history and landscape.
- Identify internal and external political resources.
- Get to know your contract lobbyist(s).
- Evaluate the wisdom and efficacy of making political contributions.
- Make the rounds.
- Learn the numbers.
- Build constituent teams.
- Become a social media ghost.
- Pick up the phone.
- Navigate internal politics.

But first, let's reconsider the earlier *pre-hire* questions for job seekers:

- Who do you want to be in your organization?
- Are you strong enough to avoid burnout?
- How government affairs sophisticated is your employer?
- How committed is your employer to an effective government affairs program?
- How committed is your employer to you?
- Can you do well in a logical but often wholly irrational environment?
- Are you prepared to protect your integrity and your dignity?

If you answered these *before you took the job*, then your employment rests on a firmer foundation. If you didn't, you can still tackle these questions. But in either case, the principle remains: *If you don't define yourself, then others will define you, shaping you into someone you may not like, but likely, someone who isn't you.* These answers are the stars to which you will navigate your career, although as a new hire you may have to pursue them subtly, if doggedly.

Let's get to your next steps.

Read 70 Experts Share Their Best Advocacy Planning, Strategy, Skills and Training Tips, by Ann Dermody. Ann writes, "We conducted 70, (yes, 70!) interviews with some of the leading minds in the worlds of government relations, lobbying, public affairs, nonprofit, advocacy, public policy, grassroots and fundraising, and asked them four pertinent questions . . . The conclusion is a taster of some of the best advocacy strategies, tips and tricks they've learned from many collective years toiling in the world of legislation and advocacy." Her "taster" is your first step; to be followed by in depth formal training.[58]

Bolster yourself with training and supplemental resources. OK, this sounds self-serving on my part, but it's true. Even if you have gotten the formal academic training I mention above, avail yourself to *Lobby School* seminars, live or online, and get our several books. This hands-on, how-to training will jump-start your career as a lobbyist and enhance your existing knowledge base. A recent law school graduate wrote to me, "And thank you for such an educational and useful class. Told my boss it was by far the most practical and useful career development course I've taken."

Plus, it will make you a more trusted counselor or consumer of contract lobbying services. If part of a team, you will show decisive leadership by suggesting these materials to your team leader for developing a common foundation for group lobbying. In all likelihood, team members learned "seat of the pants" lobbying by responding to pressures each faced at the moment but have never had time to develop a coherent overarching approach.

Learn your employer's political history and landscape. Presumably, your employer has a political history. It will help or harm your chances of lobbying success, and you need to know what it is. What is its reputation in the capitol - with lawmakers, legislative and agency staffs, other special interests, and the governor? Sometimes, your new employer, by intent or omission, doesn't disclose and so you have to ask or learn it the hard way.

To illustrate, our district's lawmaker's rudeness shocked me until *by accident* I came across an eye-opening article in the *Wall Street Journal.* The article revealed that my principal's former CEO *in the pages of the WSJ* publicly disrespected the congressman for his work trying to help my employer. However, no one had disclosed to me his hostility, thereby greatly harming my effort to secure the congressman's support. On my next lobbying visit, I acknowledged my management's insult. I profusely apologized explaining to the congressman my new management's appreciation for what he had tried to do and invited him to visit our facility. He accepted my apology and took me into the private congressional lounge where he introduced me to House members who eventually became cosponsors of my bill. Later he visited our facility, we had pictures taken with our mascot and management and all was well again between constituent and representative.

History includes political or policy positions taken by your employer. Check the political contributions made by your offi-

cers and political action committee, if any, as those may help
or hurt your lobbying. Your management, predecessor(s), and
contract lobbyist, if any, can help you.

Identify internal and external political resources. Longhand for
this is: calculate your chances of lobbying success by estimating
the plus-minus impact of your bill's supporting and opposing
political forces, internal and external. This calculation approx-
imates your employer's political strength which is roughly
proportional to your chances of winning your issue. There are
many elements with varying coefficients in this process, but the
general process can be described by the following equation:

$$\sum (+/- \text{ Power internal factors})$$
$$\underline{-\sum (+/- \text{ Power external factors})}$$

if $\sum$ +, continue lobbying

if $\sum$ −, wait until time is more favorable

That is, look at what's going for and against you in your nom-
inally controllable sphere, internal factors, and then subtract
what's going for and against you in the capital, the external
factors. To illustrate internal factors, let's consider intra-inter-
est group consensus. Group consensus is the foundation of a
successful campaign. Your group's agreement is high, so good.
On the other hand, your members live in districts whose lawmakers are largely irrelevant to the fate of this particular bill,
not so good.

Do the same for external factors. To illustrate, many special
interests will lose money if your bill becomes law, which is bad.
On the other hand, your bill advances the legislative session's
theme as agreed to by both chambers and the governor, which
is good. All this is explained in my seminars and books. By
doing this at the start, you can estimate whether your principal

should go forward this session or wait for a more favorable set of circumstances. If your principal, however, insists on going to the legislature, then you know what to do to improve your chances of winning and demonstrating you are a good hire.

Get to know your contract lobbyist(s). If your organization's contract lobbyist has been working for your new employer for any length of time, then you are either a threat or a promise to his or her economic and professional wellbeing. This is one of your most important meetings; treat it with care, confidence, and prepare. You only get one chance to make a first impression.

"At your first meeting, your lobbyist assesses your ability to manage your campaign. If you appear competent, he or she will respect you and want to work with you. If the lobbyist concludes you are in over your head, then some will be happy to hold your hand, some will cultivate your dependence upon them, others will try to wrest management of your issue away from you, and a few will exploit you."[59]

Evaluate the wisdom and efficacy of making political contributions. This goes for your employer and for you. Wright Andrews, former head of the American League of Lobbyists said, "Most of the money that has influence is not political contributions but is the money spent through lobbying, through grassroots lobbying, through newspaper advertising . . . That's what has influence."[60] Money doesn't buy votes although donors often *think* otherwise.

While new to the job and your principal's giving (or not giving) culture is well established, by examining the voting records of lawmakers to whom your company's PAC, union, or officers have given money and the amount of donations, you can estimate the cost-benefit of those donations. Or you may look at lawmakers who matter to your principal and conclude that donating to them would be a good way to keep a friend in power or at least support the party that most advances policies beneficial to your principal. However, making campaign contributions is risky business because, if you donate to a losing candidate, the winner may become your enemy.

You aren't going to change the donating culture immediately nor necessarily need to, but your knowledge of this topic expressed at just the right moment will establish your value as a government affairs counselor and value to your principal. You are new to the tribe, likely young, with little gravitas, so speak respectfully and humbly and cite your references, such as *Insiders Talk: Professional edition*. Do the work and await your moment. *It is better to prepare and the opportunity never comes, than to be unprepared when it does.*[61]

Make the rounds: You are a salesperson, not selling shoes, but selling legislation. And, like all sales people, you first sell yourself in order to sell your product. A potential customer who feels good about you *as a person* is more likely to buy from you. And you get people to feel good about you by getting to know them on a face-to-face, one-to-one, person-to-person human interaction. Recall two earlier rules, *Let your face be seen* and *Likeability is Job #1*. You have to be known to be likable and likable to get in the door; and then you have to be near to make the sale. In other words, to do your job, in order to sell, you have to "make the rounds" both during session and off-session.

During session, you make the rounds by being seen *every day* in the legislature. If your bill is being discussed and you are not there, then lawmakers may presume you no longer care, so they won't care either. You can't do this on your iPad, you have to be there.

Off-session, you make the rounds by traveling the state visiting lawmakers in their unhurried moments while comfortable back home in their districts. You meet with special interests, friends and foes, getting to know them. You visit with agency legislative liaisons. You are the new lobbyist, you personally don't have any negative baggage, and being the new lobbyist you are making a new start. This is a volatile business; just because you're opponents on this issue doesn't mean you can't work together on the next issue. Make that clear to all. Lobbyists are like the politicians with whom they work. Lord Chesterfield said, "Politicians neither love nor hate. Interest, not sentiment, directs them."

Meet with local lawmakers, city and county commissioners, aldermen, and the like. They can be useful to you as you later build home-folk constituent relationships and organize constituent advocacy groups. Ask to speak at the local rotary club or union hall about topics in which your listeners might be interested.

However, many people, but especially younger ones, are hesitant to pick up the phone and call strangers, even in their positions as lobbyists. I regularly get emails asking for visits, but without the human touch. I no more respond to them than I do to robocalls. A partner in one of America's largest multistate lobbying firms once said to me regarding his millennial staff, "Why can't they just pick up the phone?" Emails and texts seldom open doors. Once the door is opened, texts are fine, but to open it you have to be there in person.

Learn the numbers. A silk-stocking Tallahassee lobbyist advises, "Learn the numbers. What numbers drive the process you're in, state, federal or local? Know the numbers. Who terms out when? How much does a candidate have to raise? How much should I charge? These are all numbers and most lobbyists are verbal and miss the metrics part of the business."

Build constituent support. No lobbyist beats the home-folk when it comes to getting lawmakers' votes. Former Tennessee Speaker of the Senate Ron Ramsey said, "In politics, the voter is always right."[62]

The pharmaceutical industry's Patient Advocacy Groups (PAGs) consist of people who coalesce around a particular disease to advocate broadly for its treatment. Pharmaceutical representatives assist these groups with relevant information. They present themselves first as patient advocates and then as sellers of particular products. Help first, sell later.

You similarly should propose to your management that you should travel the state organizing groups around your particular issue. As with the PAGs, you are there to inform the home-folk and provide non-partisan information that they would find useful. You are there to sell yourself, and then let them know your principal understands their concerns and is a ready source of helpful information. Helping without trying to sell a product directly is also the foundation of modern marketing.

This sounds more intimidating than it really is because only 10 to 20 percent of lawmakers are important to your issue. They are on committees of jurisdiction and perhaps leadership. This means that only 10 to 20 percent of legislative districts will matter to your organizing efforts.

Become a social media ghost. A Washington, D.C. lobbyist advises, "A good lobbyist is like a CIA agent. If we've done our job, nobody knows our name."[63] Lawmakers, not lobbyists, should be in the public eye. More pointedly a senior lobbyist says,

I'm a virtual ghost online. I have a Facebook, a Twitter account and LinkedIn. But I rarely post, and certainly never about anything political or controversial. After almost twenty years in this field, I don't regret my decision at all. The corporate communications department of the company is supposed to be the public face and voice, not the lobbyist, and I liked it that way.[64]

Pick up the phone. Relationships are the foundation of trust and the human element is central to building relationships. You can't do it via electronic media. I repeat myself because it's that important. You are a competitor or ally and everyone in the capitol has to know who you are. You are introducing yourself, not cold-calling to sell an unwanted product.

An owner of a smaller lobbying firm says, "You make good points as to the time it takes and the little things that need to be done to be successful such as the phone call and that the relationship takes time. I'm not sure that young people are going to comprehend the amount of time needed to cultivate relationships that can pay dividends in the future. I think it is a bit like starting and being disciplined to contribute to a 401K or some other retirement fund."

Navigate internal politics. Finally, whether it's as a lobbyist or a store clerk and every other job, you have to work the office politics. Dr. Fredric Neuman, M.D., wrote an article advising new hires on what they need to do to navigate office politics in *"It's Not What You Know. It's Who You Know," Whose fault is that?*[65] He begins his article, "I like to think that competence is the most important determinant of professional success; but if it is, it is only over the long run." He discusses incompetent people who have great careers.

After much useful guidance, Dr. Neuman concludes his article, "Take these suggestions and someday people will admire you for the people you know in the company." And almost in passing he ends, "Aim for competence, also." Read his article and some of the many others found on the Internet and in bookstores all leading to the same conclusion that, especially in a people business like lobbying, relationships will carry you farther than professional competency, although having both is better.

Conclusion

Lobbying is a great job for those who enjoy power, influence, politics, interesting people and even working for a cause. However, in order to decide if lobbying is for you, consider the costs and benefits of being a lobbyist and decide if you are willing to pay the price. Once you do, then start looking for a job.

While on the one hand finding a job in lobbying can be difficult, on the other hand there are thousands of potential employers. But *before looking for a job* you must prepare yourself by broadly defining who you want to be in the lobbying world. Being ethical, surviving the working conditions, and navigating the people are foundational to making lobbying a career.

On your first day on the job, within limitations of the workplace, you must try to define yourself. This is done by having an agenda and knowing what needs to be done to be an effective lobbyist. Even if your employer isn't fully aware of what needs to be done, you are and you will try to nudge it in the right direction.

Best Wishes

Lobbying can be a fun and rewarding career, *if you do it right*. It's your responsibility to do it right. The contributors to this work have shown you the basics to getting and having a successful career in legislative advocacy.

The defining moment in my overall successful career wasn't going to a Finnish castle lobbying the OECD, or meeting governors or members of Congress, or even Boards of Director bonuses and plaques. It was a ceremony marking enactment of Tennessee's *Long Term Care Community Choices Act*.

The act enabled eligible Medicaid recipients to stay in their own homes rather than being institutionalized. Working that bill I learned that especially the elderly often prefer spending their last years in familiar surroundings.

At the ceremony, amongst the dignitaries and speeches, I stood beside an elderly woman in a wheelchair. Unnoticed by me, she was looking at my face. I happened to glance toward her; our eyes met. As I introduced myself, I thought, for the first time in my career I had done something more than make corporations richer. I was looking into the sparkling eyes of a real person whose life was going to be enriched from my advocacy. My lobbying made a difference for her, as at that moment, she did for me.

I wish you the best in your lobbying career. It can be fun, well paying, test you, and even make you a better person. And perhaps by your lobbying you too will make a real difference in someone's life. Let me know when you do.

Robert L. Guyer   www.lobbyschool.com
The Lobby School   rlguyer@lobbyschool.com

Appendix 1: Can Working in an Election Campaign Help Me Achieve My Legislative Goals?

Roger Austin, Ph.D., Esq. and Robert L. Guyer, Esq.
(Revised February 12, 2019)

This article addresses a very specific question: *Does working in election campaigns present opportunities to build relationships with candidates that will increase your ability to more successfully lobby them once elected?* To answer this question, we will consider three elements: 1) potential future benefit from working in an election campaign; 2) mechanism for effectively doing so; and, 3) making your investment pay off legislatively.

Why Work in an Election Campaign?

While people work in campaigns for various reasons as discussed below, for our purposes we are there to develop *friendships* with the candidate and those likely to be the lawmaker's advisors or even staff, should he or she win. You may have heard, "Politicians take care of their friends." By working in an election campaign, you become a friend and accrue the candidate's political goodwill. You hope that the friendship and goodwill you gain will motivate the lawmaker to reward you with an increment of access and support for your political goals.

After President Bill Clinton was inaugurated, Washington, D.C. was filled with people wearing large buttons simply proclaiming, "FOB", that is, "Friend of Bill." In those early heady days, being an FOB held considerable cachet in Washington.[66] Your expectation is that the cache you gain as friends of lawmakers will bolster your influence with special interests, and lawmakers and their staffs.

And you might find it fun and educational. There is nothing quite like being in the trenches to see campaigning close-up, *as it really is*. You will see the grueling reality of the campaign process, and its agonies and successes. Involvement at this level with a candidate not only shows you things you have never seen before, it will also give you a greater empathy for what a candidate must endure. This can be an exhilarating experience!

THE RAPID EVOLUTION OF MODERN ELECTION CAMPAIGNS

Campaigning is rapidly changing because *the way people vote* is changing. In Washington, Oregon, and Colorado elections are solely voting by mail ("VBM") and 39 states offer early voting ("EV").[67] Pre-election voting, VBM and EV, is collectively referred to as *convenience voting* ("CV"). CV allows voters to cast their ballots how and when they want. We leave to other authors to discuss the merits and dangers of convenience voting.[68, 69]

To illustrate the CV trend, Florida in 2014 marked the first time over 50% of voters voted before Election Day - 30% VBM and 22% EV. In 2016, CV topped 60% and in 2018 it was over 65%. The net effect is that today there are 3 different election campaigns – VBM, EV, and regular old fashioned get out the vote ("GOTV") on the last weekend. Each of these phases can capture 1/3 of votes cast.

Modern election campaigns are far more complex than the simple GOTV of earlier days. CV has major implications for campaigns, especially when and how expenditures of resources and money and positions for volunteers are made. These changes create broader and at the same time more specialized opportunities for campaign workers.

FOR WHICH PARTICULAR CANDIDATES SHOULD I WORK?

There are many reasons for your choosing to work for a specific candidate - affinity with him or her, political platform, empathy for your issue or organization, constituency, perception the candidate will win, and of course, your own political advancement. However, your motive is to work for candidates selected for their potential future legislative value to you, your organization, and your issues.

Identifying candidates with future legislative value is a matter of judgment, as are most political decisions. When evaluating *incumbents*, future value is estimated by looking at their records. Are they currently serving on committees of jurisdiction over your issues or in chamber or party leadership? Have they voted favorably on your concerns in the past? Do you expect their party to be in the majority next legislature? What are their current campaigns promising and to whom?

When considering *challengers* or *candidates for an open seat*, again look at their records. Evaluate their positions taken on matters similar to yours. Determine how favorable their political parties are to your kinds of issues. Consider how the political environment of their districts may be favorable or unfavorable to your position. Finally, identify the campaign promises they are making and the individuals or groups who may benefit from those promises.

First time candidates find that their first endorsement is the one most difficult to get. Whoever gives that first endorsement to a candidate, who later is elected, will be in a powerful position for future lobbying. But on the other hand, if your candidate fails you will have to bear the consequences.

EYES WIDE OPEN: CAN I AFFORD TO LOSE MY BET?

Working in electoral campaigns can have good cost-benefit payouts. That's the nature of especially high-stakes gambling. However, keep in mind that you are playing with the powerful. Giving any kind of open political support, taking any kind of political position, is *risky business*. "But if you bet and lose [on a candidate], you will be on the winning candidate's list of foes, and this can have long-term negative consequences. Never underestimate a lawmaker's petulance and desire for revenge. For example, a legislator may refuse to support your bill or may work against you because you supported his or her opponent(s) in the past."[70]

Further, supporting a challenger against an incumbent *multiplies* the already existing hazards of getting involved in elections in general. Incumbents have high rates of staying in office; for example, in 2018 state lawmakers had a 91 percent reelection rate.[71] Consequently, it is easy to see why challengers find it difficult to get people to place their bets on them. And at the same time, it is also easy to see why so many people flock to support incumbents.

Grossly speaking, the odds of a challenger winning against an incumbent are so low that if he or she wins, then you win big. However, if the odds go as expected and the incumbent wins, you will lose big. Perhaps, even the pre-election favor you may have enjoyed earlier may be replaced with *life-long hostility*.

Your options *in order of increasing probability of winning your bet* are to:

- Support challengers against incumbents.
- For open seats, support candidates from the party opposing the former lawmaker.
- For open seats, support candidates of the same party as the former lawmaker.
- Support incumbents.

Or win nothing and lose nothing by sitting out the election. But even this may be hazardous to former supporters because the lawmaker may conclude your non-support means you are no longer friends; not a declared enemy, but certainly no longer a friend.

WHAT KINDS OF SUPPORT CAN I LEGALLY GIVE?

There many ways to support candidates. These include cash or in-kind contributions, placing a sign in your yard or bumper sticker on your car, attending "meet-and-greet" receptions, attending fundraisers, rallying friends, relatives, neighbors and co-workers to vote, and making favorable Facebook, Instagram, and social media posts. These quick and easy contributions are similar in that they are indirect and generally indistinguishable from identical contributions being made by many others. But while the preceding activities are valuable, volunteering in a campaign is unique *as to becoming a friend.*

Working as a campaign volunteer is direct, tangible to the candidate, and immediately distinguishes you from those who contributed indirectly. Working on a campaign also takes much more time and personal investment.

Sometimes people or organizations choose to "hedge their bets" by donating to both incumbent and challenger. They may even place volunteers on both candidates' campaigns. However, lawmakers are looking for friends. Upon finding out that a group is not a true friend but is playing both sides to *hedge its bets*, lawmakers may refuse the group the political favor it was trying to secure. In the book *Speaking Freely* former U.S. senator Slade Gorton says, "It just seems to me that those who were trying to buy influence on both sides were simply wasting their money . . . The idea that you can play both sides and have people like you, or influence them, I think is an extremely foolish one."[72]

Volunteers, especially committed volunteers, are hard to find and keep. Because of other commitments in life, it is difficult to locate volunteers who will show up, much less work diligently on a regular basis. Election campaigns are usually desperate to find reliable people who will do what they say and then follow through consistently. Those who show up frequently, consistently, and who deliver what they promise can rise to prominent positions in campaigns, even after a few short weeks or months.

Experienced campaigners expect that some volunteers will fail to deliver what they promise. However, this does not mean that they will be forgiving when confronting a volunteer who has failed to honor his or her commitments. A volunteer who promises less but who is faithful will be better perceived and gain more than one who promises more but proves unfaithful.

Further, elected officials and their staffs also remember campaign volunteers who made promises and then did not deliver. Since effective lobbying is founded on trustworthiness, a record of faithlessness may greatly hamper the lackadaisical volunteer's and their organization's future lobbying credibility and effectiveness.

What Can I Do Specifically for the Candidate's Campaign?

After deciding the candidates you will support, next consider, what you can do for them. What do I have to offer? What are the available transferable resources within my organization?

Let's start with you supplying personnel. More than likely, you will be associated with a group. You must determine who among your group to involve. In reality, only half of those who claim they will work in a campaign will actually do so. Once you have identified those interested in working with a campaign, ask your volunteers for firm commitments of their time. Then, discount the time they have committed by half. These two steps will provide a realistic estimate of your resources, volunteers and time available, that you can offer to election campaigns. With this estimate in hand, you can better assess how many, if any, campaign(s) in which you can work and with what concrete tasks you are equipped to help.

Next, what can your volunteers do? Although the list is virtually unlimited, below is a short overview of activities for you to consider:

- Help target precinct-specific activity or set voter turnout goals.

- Walk precincts - candidates talk more about walking precincts than they actually do. Walking is long, hard, slow, and often sweaty work. Some neighbors will be welcoming and others rude; be prepared. If you or your group can give a full morning or afternoon to walking precincts, or better yet, walk 3–4 times, you will truly distinguish yourself.

- Organize a surprise traffic blitz - campaigns need to keep volunteers on the street corners for the entire election period, crescendoing three days before Election Day. Since all candidates are involved with this activity, organize your groups to be on 10 to 12 major intersections at the start of convenience voting. Being early will leave you with roads that have little competition, and if planned correctly, all drivers will see you no matter where they are going throughout the morning or afternoon. This strategy may bring your candidate to the attention of unaware or undecided voters and may also help you get news coverage - the equivalent of free advertising.

- Manage pre-election day voting – as mentioned above, most voting today is CV. VBM has to be fanned. EV may have you standing for two weeks outside of an early voting station to remind voters about your candidate. For CV you can help the campaign "track" early voters to avoid wasting GOTV time where votes have been cast. During the last few days of the campaign this lets the campaign focus on the 35% of votes still to be gotten.

- Ballot harvesting is legal in some states. In it groups rely on data showing which voters requested absentee ballots but have not turned them in. They then go door-to-door and offer to collect and turn in those ballots for the voters—often dozens or hundreds at a time. Some place ballot-collection boxes in high-concentration voter areas, such as college campuses, and then take the ballots to election offices when the boxes are full.[73]

- Maintain the candidate's website, track hits, and respond to email requests;

- Direct a campaign to write letters to the editor in local newspapers, political websites, and blogs. Contribute as a "ghost" writer or help other supporters by editing their articles to ensure a consistent and coherent message.

- Place signs in your yard or spread the bigger signs throughout the community and log their locations.

- Maintain the database of financial records.

- Prepare state-required financial reports that list contributions and expenditures. Although tedious and at times maddening, it is extremely important to maintain and submit accurate reports on time. Involvement with this task, will give you an early sense of those who have the lawmaker's attention - important information to know if he or she is elected to the legislature.

- Work with the supervisor of elections to maintain the candidate's list of those who have voted by mail in order to contact them to ensure they vote but then not annoy them with continuing contacts. VBM can constitute a large percent of voters. For example, in Florida, "Two years ago, 29 percent of all ballots cast in the presidential election were cast by mail—2.7 million out of about 9.6 million ballots—and election experts say the rate may be higher this November."[74]

- Help at headquarters - with the exception of million dollar races that have paid staff and a center of operations, most state and local campaigns do not have campaign headquarters in the sense of a storefront. Most state and local campaigns, in fact, are run from the candidates' homes, garages, or offices.

- Campaign headquarters need people to assist with menial tasks that often take huge amounts of time, activities such as organizing and cleaning the headquarters, opening mail, logging donors and their contributions, preparing campaign reports, preparing "thank you" notes, organizing precinct walks, answering telephones, and assembling yard and car-top signs.

Remember, election campaigns always need committed and reliable workers. There are usually more things to be done than there are hours in the day. Your job is to identify a campaign that advances your interests and that fits your politics, talents, and available time. Some of the activities listed, especially those with a computer orientation, can be completed at your home or office. A teenager or college student with an interest in politics may also complete these activities.

THE VALUE OF "FACE" TIME

Most importantly for your purposes, working in a campaign provides opportunity to spend quality time with a candidate, his or her family, and staff at an enormously stressful time in their lives. While you are building relationships and making meaningful campaign contributions, you are also sowing seeds that will grow into opportunity for future lobbying.

When candidates are in their campaign headquarters, it is easy to contact them. Throughout the campaign, you must use every opportunity to personally associate with the candidate, his or her personal staff, and most importantly the candidate's family and close friends. To have future influence, you must distinguish yourself and your labors from those of the other volunteers. You must always be polite, supportive, helpful, and in the candidate's field of vision.

Finally, the human relationship you build with a candidate can be golden. You will always remember your contribution to his or her success and feel a sense of involvement and pride when seeing the lawmaker in the supermarket or on television. He or she has become your friend.

The Legislative Rewards of Volunteering

On election night you will either be part of a *thrill of victory* party or commiserating with losers in *the agony of defeat*. A loss can crush a lawmaker's soul. Watch on YouTube the 2016 pain of Secretary Clinton and her supporters to get a sense of certainty turning into disbelief, grief, and loss. Then watch the joy of President Trump and his supporters. All this can be quite emotional, win or lose.

Once Election Day has passed, the newly elected or reelected lawmakers will be sworn in and they will prepare for the upcoming organizational and legislative sessions. You should attend their swearing-in ceremonies.

Now, just as you helped your candidates win elections, you are now in a position to help them as lawmakers achieve *their legislative goals*. By helping them in ways that also benefit yourself, you will continue to show yourself a friend to the lawmaker.

Further, you have learned the souls of your lawmakers – what they really think, what they feel, what their passions are, what motivates them. You know their families and associates. You know their supporters and voters. You know their districts' needs. Your intimate knowledge gives you insights into fashioning legislative packages that they can find attractive. It's through your volunteering that you gained political intelligence that gives you a step up over your capitol competition.

Does this mean that you will get special treatment or win every issue? The answer is "no." However, by having invested your heart, money, time, and other resources in the election campaign you have opened the door to cement a political relationship with a lawmaker. Knowing that you worked in his or her campaign, the lawmaker should be more receptive to you, your organization, and issues because you have proven yourself to be a *friend*.

LONG-TERM REWARDS OF WORKING IN ELECTION CAMPAIGNS

Even if your candidate lost, you are still the richer for you have learned much and may have made a friend with the candidate and supporters. You worked with the losing candidate because he or she offered you more potential support than the eventual winner. And if the loss was in a close vote, your candidate may try again, especially if the seat will be open next election.[75]

If the winner is angry with you, try to build a better relationship. You need not be lifetime enemies. "I say this realizing with some lawmakers you will never have a rapport, but you can improve your relationships. Civil relationships are in all parties' interests, and neither you nor the lawmaker knows when you might unexpectedly agree. If your principal operates in a lawmaker's district, building relationships is easier and more natural."[76]

Another benefit from working on election campaigns is, over successive campaign cycles, you grow in election experience and expertise. At the beginning, you may only have enough time and talent to support one or two campaigns. However, as you and your group work through successive campaign cycles, you will become more adept at using your resources. In time you may be able to add to the numbers of elections campaigns your group can support.

Over the longer term, you will develop a niche and perhaps, expertise in key areas of election campaigning - for example, voter targeting, precinct walking, VBM, EV, and GOTV. If you develop a reputation for delivering what you promise on time, word will travel and you could begin to receive requests from future candidates.

Your group's influence with legislators will grow as you contribute labor, time, and money to election campaigns. Your "sweat equity" donations will continue to distinguish your group from others, especially those who have nothing better to give than just money. By working in election campaigns, you build political relationships, credits, and lawmaker awareness of you, and your expertise. These will be invaluable in future legislative lobbying endeavors.

As with anything else in life, remember that the sun always rises in the morning – win or lose there is *a day after.* And as long as there is a United States of America, there will be future election campaigns to work and lawmaker relationships to build. Enjoy the process and reap the rewards.

ABOUT ROGER AUSTIN

Roger Austin is a Gainesville, Florida-based political consultant and a serial graduate of the University of Florida (including a J.D. received from the Levin College of Law). After serving as political director and legal counsel for the Republican Party of Florida from 1989–92, he moved into the private sector and started his own firm in 1996. He has consulted with candidates for state and local office in all parts of Florida. Working between campaign cycles, Austin completed his Ph.D. in Political Science at the University of Florida in 2015; his dissertation was titled *Patterns of Failure–Rethinking Campaign Finance Reform: What Went Wrong?* He also teaches classes in campaign management for the Graduate Program in Political Campaigning and teaches a variety of undergraduate political science classes, as well.

ABOUT ROBERT GUYER

Robert Guyer lobbied at the state, federal, and international legislative and administrative levels, both as an in-house and contract lobbyist. He has been teaching effective lobbying skills since 2002 as part of the *Lobby School*. Select publications include:

- *Guide to State Legislative Lobbying*, editions 1–3
- *How to Successfully Lobby State Legislatures, Guide to State Legislative Lobbying 4ᵗʰ edition*
- *Insiders Talk: Winning with Lobbyists, Professional edition*
- *Insiders Talk: Winning with Lobbyists, Readers edition*
- *Insiders Talk: Glossary of Legislative Concepts and Representative Terms*

- *The Campaign Method for More Effective State Government Affairs,* 15-part video series, www.lobbyschool.com

A graduate of the University of Florida he holds degrees in political science, civil engineering, and law; and is admitted to the practice of law in Florida and the District of Columbia. You may learn more about him, the *Lobby School,* and effective advocacy techniques at www.lobbyschool.com. You may contact him at rlguyer@lobbyschool.com or through the website www.lobbyschool.com.

Appendix 2: Effective Lobbying Is Getting Votes! 27 Fundamentals for Successful Lobbying

1. Your threshold question for each lawmaker is, "Why would this lawmaker give me his or her vote?" Until you can answer that question, you are not likely to get the vote.

2. Your answer is, "Because I have what this lawmaker wants." If you don't, go home.

3. Lawmakers are your "customers." Customers buy to meet their needs, not yours.

4. The more you look like your customer, the more likely you'll make the sale.

5. Lawmakers are not like you - and the longer they're in office the less they're like you.

6. Winning a lawmaker's vote is 10% access and 90% heat. Access is easy. "Political heat" is a few active higher-level constituents, both in- and out-of-district.

7. Get past "nice" to get lawmakers' votes. A lawmaker's being nice isn't a vote.

8. "Lobbying is a dance of seduction." Find and use each lawmaker's susceptibilities.

9. "Facts don't vote." A lawmaker votes his or her own peculiar political calculus. Seldom are technical facts enough to get votes; but political facts may be all it takes.

10. 70% of winning a lawmaker's vote occurs before talking to the lawmaker.

11. Lawmakers are almost wholly motivated by special interests. Lobby the special interests that put and keep a lawmaker in power before you lobby that lawmaker.

12. 80–90% of lawmakers are irrelevant to your winning or losing your bill. The relevant ones are on key committees; plus the few, if any, other lawmakers who actually care.

13. Convince relevant lawmakers to partner with you. You must show each why working with you is good for him or her, politically. "Self-interest is the engine of government."

14. Most lawmakers' votes are won or lost at fish fries, not in committee meetings.

15. Most committee meetings are theater since the votes were committed at the fish fry.

16. "The lower you shoot, the higher you hit." Lobby staff, then members of the committee of first reference, its chair, then gatekeeper committees. Lobby leadership last, if at all.

17. There is no unimportant staff. You may not need a staff person's support, but you can't afford his or her opposition. Build warm relationships with staff!

18. The more work you do for lawmakers and especially staff the more likely your ideas will become law. Materials that don't help them do their jobs end up in the trash!

19. Legislatures operate on 3 types of rules: 1) written; 2)

unwritten; 3) unwritten and unspoken. Violate any of the 3 and you will be disrespected as being ill-informed.

20. Unwritten rule 1- you have to talk to people you don't like, and who don't like you.

21. Unwritten and unspoken rule 1- "Thou shalt make campaign contributions" to be a long-term capitol player. Money is good; constituent support better; both is best.

22. Coalitions are indispensable. They exist for advantage - not for love, loyalty, or debt. Don't pre-qualify or disqualify a potential partner. "Politics makes strange bedfellows."

23. Most contract lobbyists have little personal political power. Don't confuse a lobbyist's ability to say "hi" to a lawmaker with the ability to get that lawmaker's vote.

24. Your contract lobbyist should be a better lobbyist for the legislature overall. Your members should be better lobbyists for their districts' lawmakers.

25. The best time to lobby is when you don't need anything.

26. Agencies promulgate 90% of laws. This means what the legislature giveth an agency can taketh away; and what the legislature wouldn't give you an agency might.

27. Nobody cares about your issue as much as you do. Neither money nor the best contractors can win your battles for you. If you don't make it happen, then it won't.

ENDNOTES

1   "How to become a Lobbyist," *Career Explorer* (accessed February 15, 2019) https://www.careerexplorer.com/careers/lobbyist/how-to-become/.

2   T. R. Goldman, "Forget creativity: Can lobbying be taught?," *The Washington Post* (November 18, 2012) https://goo.gl/D2khji.

3   How to Become a Lobbyist," *Norwich University* (December 13, 2018) https://online.norwich.edu/academic-programs/resources/how-become-lobbyist.

4   "Our" because everything I write relies on comments and feedback from other lobbyists.

5   A fairly typical definition of lobbying is, "[I]nfluencing or attempting to influence legislative action or non-action through oral or written communication or an attempt to obtain the goodwill of a member or employee of the legislature." § 11.045(e), Fla. Stat. (2017).

6   Rich Cranwell, Director of Governmental Relations, American Healthcare, LLC (Richmond, Virginia), email communication with author, October 14, 2019.

7   "Lobbying in Texas, A Guide to the Texas Law," *Texas Ethics Commission* (October 1, 2019) https://www.ethics.state.tx.us/data/resources/guides/lobby_guide.pdf.

8   Megan Brenan, "Nurses Keep Healthy Lead as Most Honest, Ethical Profession," *Gallup* (December 26, 2017) https://news.gallup.com/poll/224639/nurses-keep-healthy-lead-honest-ethical-profession.aspx. "While only members of Congress [11%] and lobbyists [8%] received majority negative ratings..." in "Ameri-

cans' Ratings of Honesty and Ethical Standards in Professions," December 4-11, 2017.

9   Nurses Keep Healthy Lead as Most Honest, Ethical Profession.

10   Goldman repeats this concept in "Forget creativity: Can lobbying be taught? I recall hearing it years earlier than his article, suggesting the expression has been around for many years.

11   Jimmy Williams, "I was a lobbyist for more than 6 years. I quit. My conscience couldn't take it anymore," *Vox* (January 15, 2018) https://www.vox.com/first-person/2017/6/29/15886936/political-lobbying-lobbyist-big-money-politics.

12   State Sen. Uvalde Lindsey (D, Fayetteville, AR), personal conversation with author, December 18, 2014.

13   Roxana Tiron, "Bipartisanship a key to success," *The Hill* (September 08, 2005) https://thehill.com/business-a-lobbying/2783-bipartisanship-a-key-to-success.

14   "Aptitude," *Dictionary.com* (accessed October 25, 2019) https://www.dictionary.com/browse/aptitude.

15   Forget creativity: Can lobbying be taught?

16   "Making it as a Lobbyist in Washington, D.C.," *The Washington Center* (October 29, 2013) https://www.twc.edu/articles/making-it-lobbyist-washington-dc.

17   "Perseverence," *Dictionary.com* (accessed December 1, 2019) https://www.dictionary.com/browse/perseverance.

18   "State Legislatures vs. Congress: Which Is More Productive?," *Quora* (accessed April 2, 2019) https://www.

INSIDERS TALK: HOW TO GET AND KEEP YOUR FIRST LOBBYING JOB

quorum.us/data-driven-insights/state-legislatures-ver-
sus-congress-which-is-more-productive/176/.

19 Mid-Atlantic lobbyist, this manuscript review comments, July 9, 2019.

20 Forget creativity: Can lobbying be taught?

21 Sophia Mitrokostas, "10 benefits of being attractive,
according to science," *Insider* (Dec. 7, 2018) https://
www.thisisinsider.com/benefits-of-being-attrac-
tive-science-2018-12.

22 I first heard "facts don't vote" from Florida House staff
Ron Phillips who at the time also was a graduate student in the lobbying class I taught at Florida State University. As of this writing Ron is President and CEO
of Republic Consultants, LLC, and of-counsel to Gavel
Resources, both Washington, D.C. lobbying firms.

23 "Average Entry-Level Lobbyist Salary," *PayScale*
(accessed September 24, 2019) https://www.payscale.
com/research/US/Job=Lobbyist/Salary/46149334/
Entry-Level.

24 "Lobbyist Salary in the United States," Salary.com
(accessed September 24, 2019) https://www.salary.com/
research/salary/benchmark/lobbyist-salary#viewsalary.

25 Making it as a lobbyist in Washington, D.C.

26 "Lobbyist Registration Information," *National Conference of State Legislatures* (accessed November 29, 2006,
no url available [2019]) – Note: 16 states do not list
numbers of principals.

27 Peggy Kearns, "A Big Business and Growing: Online
Extra for the Influence Business," *National Conference of*

State Legislatures (January 2009) http://www.National Conference of State Legislatures.org/research/ethics/lobbying-a-big-business-and-growing.aspx.

28   These data have not been reported due to the difficulty to reconcile reporting systems used by the states. For example, some states list government employee lobbyists while most do not.

29   "Number of registered active lobbyists in the United States from 2000 to 2018," *Statista* (accessed February 15, 2019) https://www.statista.com/statistics/257340/number-of-lobbyists-in-the-us/.

30   Liz Essley Whyte and Ben Weidner, "Amid federal gridlock, lobbying rises in the states," *The Center for Public Integrity* (February 11, 2016) https://publicintegrity.org/state-politics/amid-federal-gridlock-lobbying-rises-in-the-states/.

31   *Insiders Talk: Winning with Lobbyists, Professional edition* (Engineering THE LAW, Inc.: Gainesville, 2018) discusses lobbyists and good and bad clients in detail.

32   Gina Belli/PayScale "At least 70% of jobs are not even listed — here's how to up your chances of getting a great new gig," *Business Insider* (April 10, 2017) https://www.businessinsider.com/at-least-70-of-jobs-are-not-even-listed-heres-how-to-up-your-chances-of-getting-a-great-new-gig-2017-4.

33   Chris Micheli and Rex Frazier, "So you want to be a lobbyist? Read on…" *Capitol Weekly* (November 4, 2016) https://capitolweekly.net/so-you-want-to-be-a-lobbyist/.

34   So you want to be a lobbyist? Read on…

35   "Size of state legislative staff," *National Confer-
      ence of State Legislatures* (October 2, 2018) http://
      www.National Conference of State Legislatures.
      org/research/about-state-legislatures/staff-change-
      chart-1979-1988-1996-2003-2009.aspx.

36   "The Best Digital Rolodex Apps," *Novel Coworking*
      (November 26, 2018) https://novelcoworking.com/the-
      best-digital-rolodex-apps/.

37   Naomi Lim, "Staffers-turned-lawmakers find they
      face hundreds of thousands of bosses rather than one,"
      (italic) Washington Examiner (end italic)," (July 18,
      2019)   https://www.washingtonexaminer.com/news/
      staffers-turned-lawmakers-find-they-face-hundreds-of-
      thousands-of-bosses-rather-than-one.

38   Southern state lobbyist, email to author, July 29, 2019.

39   Mid-Atlantic lobbyist.

40   Christian Britschgi, "Local Governments Spend Big
      on Lobbyists," *Reason* (August 8, 2017) https://reason.
      com/2017/08/08/local-governments-spend-big-on-lob-
      byists/.

41   California specific, "Almost 400 local government
      groups have lobbyists, and they run the gamut from
      large cities to rural counties. School districts have lobby-
      ists, too, as do some tribal governments. No level of local
      government appears to be too small: Santa Monica's rent
      control board paid $12,246 to have someone watching
      the Legislature this spring, while Sonoma County's
      parks district has paid $13,500 this year to do the same."
      John Myers, "Political Road Map: No one spends more
      on lobbying in Sacramento than local governments," *Los
      Angeles Times* (August 06, 2017) https://www.latimes.

com/politics/la-pol-ca-road-map-lobbying-local-governments-20170806-story.html. For local lobbying in general see Julia A. Payson, "Cities, Lobbyists, and Representation in Multilevel Government," (September 5, 2018) https://pdfs.semanticscholar.org/5939/8a4c2a-24ea39da1ec76a955d9e067b5e959c.pdf.

42   JD Careers Out There, "Lobbying Jobs - Careers For Lawyers in Government Relations," *YouTube* video (February 28, 2013) https://www.youtube.com/watch?v=E-JWMD5rCyqg.

43   So you want to be a lobbyist? Read on...

44   "Jobs," *Public Affairs Council* (accessed November 4, 2019) https://pac.org/jobs.

45   "Association Management Companies Factsheet," *AMC Institute* (accessed April 25, 2019) https://www.amcinstitute.org/page/industryfactsheet.

46   For example, "Just last year, Facebook lobbied the White House; the State, Justice, Commerce, Labor, Homeland Security and Housing and Urban Development departments, as well as the Federal Trade Commission, the Federal Communications Commission, the U.S Trade Representative and the Office of Science and Technology. To do this, Facebook hired 11 different lobbying firms, and paid eight of its own in-house lobbyists." Josh Keefe, "How Mark Zuckerberg and Facebook Have Spent More Than $50 Million On Influence in Washington," *Newsweek* (April 10, 2018) https://www.newsweek.com/how-facebook-exerts-influence-washington-dc-879378.

47   Barney Jopson and Joanna Kao, "Amazon builds tech's largest in-house lobbying team," *Financial Times* (April

3, 2018) https://www.ft.com/content/56ddca24-3752-11e8-8eee-e06bde01c544.

48   *Insiders Talk: Winning with Lobbyists, Professional edition,* 145.

49   Silk-stocking refers to a prestigious law or lobbying firm. Also, "Other definition of silk stocking is a contemptuous term for a politician in the 19th century in America." "Silk stocking," (italic) educalingo (end italic) (accessed December 3, 2019) https://educalingo.com/en/dic-en/silk-stocking.

50   "Seven Years into a Lawyers Career," *Researching Law* (Spring 2009) http://www.americanbarfoundation.org/uploads/cms/documents/abf_rl_spring09_final.pdf.

51   Forget creativity: Can lobbying be taught?

52   *Indeed* (accessed February 16, 2019) https://www.indeed.com/q-Political-Affairs-Intern-jobs.html/.

53   Sarah J. Eckman, "Internships in Congressional Offices: Frequently Asked Questions," *Congressional Research Service* (October 15, 2018) https://fas.org/sgp/crs/misc/R44491.pdf.

54   Saige Driver, "Keep It Clean: Social Media Screenings Gain in Popularity," *Business News Daily* (October 7, 2018) https://www.businessnewsdaily.com/2377-social-media-hiring.html.

55   Benjamin Franklin said this in the Continental Congress just before signing the Declaration of Independence, 1776. "Franklin's Contributions to the American Revolution as a Diplomat in France," *Historic Valley Forge* (accessed August 19, 2019) www.ushistory.org/

valleyforge/history/franklin.html.

56   Michael Volkov, Esq., "The Myth of the Rogue Employee," *Volkov Lawgroup, LLC* (March 29, 2016) https://blog.volkovlaw.com/2016/03/myth-rogue-employee/.

57   Ann Dermody, "70 Experts Share Their Best Advocacy Planning, Strategy, Skills and Training Tips," *Fiscal Note | CQ Roll Call* (February 1, 2019) https://fiscalnote.com/blog/70-experts-share-their-best-advocacy-planning-strategy-skills-and-training-tips.

58   Ann Dermody.

59   *Insiders Talk: Winning with Lobbyists, Professional edition,* 143.

60   Larry Mankinson, *Speaking Freely: Washington Insiders Talk About Money in Politics,* 2nd ed. (Washington, D.C.: Center for Responsive Politics, 2003), 84.

61   Franco Genarro, NCAA/NFL Sports Chaplain, Gainesville, Florida comment to author (2019).

62   Senate Speaker Ron Ramsey said this to a meeting of the Tennessee Lobbyists Association, circa 2009.

63   Government affairs manager, e-mail communication with author, August 2, 2017.

64   Mid-Atlantic lobbyist.

65   Fredric Neuman, M.D. "It's Not What You Know. It's Who You Know" Whose fault is that?" *Psychology Today* (Jun 11, 2014) https://www.psychologytoday.com/us/blog/fighting-fear/201406/its-not-what-you-know-its-who-you-know.

66   Stephan Lavaton, "The Growing List: Ex-Friends of
        Bill," *The New York Times* (April 20, 1997) 5137 https://
        www.nytimes.com/1997/04/20/weekinreview/the-
        growing-list-ex-friends-of-bill.html.

67   "Absentee and Early Voting," *National Conference of State
        Legislatures* (November 11, 2019) http://www.ncsl.org/
        research/elections-and-campaigns/absentee-and-ear-
        ly-voting.aspx.

68   "Voting by mail and absentee voting," *MIT Election
        Data + Science Lab* (accessed February 13, 2019) https://
        electionlab.mit.edu/research/voting-mail-and-absen-
        tee-voting.

69   "All-Mail Elections (AKA Vote-By-Mail)," *National
        Conference of State Legislatures,* (August 15, 2018) http://
        www.ncsl.org/research/elections-and-campaigns/all-
        mail-elections.aspx.

70   *Insiders Talk: Winning with Lobbyists, Professional edition,*
        229.

71   "Seats held by 6,073 incumbent state legislators were
        up for election in 2018. Of those, 4,952 (82 percent)
        filed for re-election. In 2018, 469 incumbents were
        defeated in primary elections and the general elections
        on November 6, 2018," "Incumbents defeated in 2018's
        state legislative elections," *Ballotpedia* (accessed Feb-
        ruary 12, 2019) https://ballotpedia.org/Incumbents_
        defeated_in_2018%27s_state_legislative_elections.

72   Larry Mankinson, *Speaking Freely: Washington Insid-
        ers Talk About Money in Politics, 2nd ed.* (Washington,
        D.C.: Center for Responsive Politics, 2003), 44.

73   "Both Political Parties Use Ballot Harvesting, But What

is (sic) It?" *Voice of America News* (December 6, 2018) https://www.voanews.com/usa/us-politics/both-politi-cal-parties-use-ballot-harvesting-what-it.

74   Steve Bousquet, "If you vote by mail in Florida, it's 10 times more likely that ballot won't count," *Miami Herald* (September 21, 2018) https://www.miamiher-ald.com/news/politics-government/state-politics/arti-cle218654810.html.

75   Simone Pathé, "To run or not to run again? Failed 2018 candidates weigh 2020 options," *Roll Call* (February 14, 2019) https://www.rollcall.com/news/campaigns/run-not-run-failed-2018-candidates-weigh-2020-op-tions?utm_source=morningheadlines&utm_medi-um=email&utm_campaign=newsletters&utm_con-tent=02/14/2019.

76   *Insiders Talk: Winning with Lobbyists, Professional edition*, 224.